Overcome by His Love

by

Craig Snyder

Table of Contents

Chapter 1   The Beginning

Chapter 2   Abiding In Him

Chapter 3   Overcome By His Love

Chapter 4   Chosen Of God

Chapter 5   Discovering The Blessings Of God

                 Through Troubles

Chapter 6   Only Believe

Chapter 7   How To Know The Will Of God

Chapter 8   Delay – Why Jesus Tarries

Chapter 9   Being A Witness

Chapter 10   Come To Me

Dedication

I want to dedicate this book to my wife, Jonni, who loves me and accepts me unconditionally. She is still the love of my life after more than forty years of marriage. Also, to my dad who is with the Lord; he now knows how much he is loved by Jesus. And to my mother who has continued to love and support me as only a mother can. Finally, to my children and grandchildren, they are the most amazing young people that I have ever known and I am so proud of them.

Preface

After many years of ministry in local churches and extensive travel in the United States and overseas, I see something that Christians world-wide have in common. When they are born again and receive the life of Christ that has been given to them from eternity past and believe that it is truly theirs, there is a joy and lightness in their life. Everything is different and they have come to know a peace within that leads to a smile on their face and skip in their step. Everyone and everything are beautiful.

I am sorry to say that this euphoria doesn't last long. Some people will say it is because they don't keep the principles that the Bible teaches. I don't think that is it at all. When I was saved, my desires changed without anyone except the Holy Spirit giving me direction. In fact, in the beginning everyone was so amazed at the change in my life, all they did was watch me. Life was great and I was having fun living my new Christian life.

People that I had known for many years began to change also. Some after watching me and realizing what had taken place in my life was real, also believed Christ and were born again. Others decided without consciously thinking about it, that this new lifestyle was not for them and pulled away from me. They still "liked" me and I them, but things were not the same and we were not close anymore. One thing I now know looking back, there was not a religious bone in my body.

I was going to church because I wanted to go. I was telling people about Jesus because it was the desire of my heart. I was reading my Bible because God spoke to me so much when I did. I could understand what He was saying and it made perfect sense to me. This is how many people start out when they are "saved".

What happens to so many people to change this? They are introduced to something that will most certainly doom them to failure. Not only will it doom them to failure, it is also unnecessary in the life of the believer. What is this thing that has caused so many Christians to live in defeat and discouragement? The thing that ultimately leads to defeat, discouragement and lack of peace in the life of a believer is religion.

Religion tells you that there is something you need to do to be right with God when God says that He has already done it. You only need to believe Him that He has done it. Religion tells you that you must keep the law to be right with God when God says that the purpose of the law was to show you how much you needed a savior and that there was no hope without Him. You couldn't live up to the law to be saved and you can't live up to the law after you are saved. I have good news for the believer, you don't have to live up to the law; Jesus did and He counted it to you. He gave you His righteousness, His position, His sonship because He wanted to. You could not have even believed Him if He had not given you the gift of faith, Ephesians 2:8,9. It is a free gift not deserved or worked for by man. You couldn't earn it but it was freely given to you.

What a great Grace gift, the ability to believe in Him.

We are going to explore who we are in Christ and just

what our position is in Him in this book. Also, it is my

desire that Christians will regain that child-like faith

that they had when they were first saved and will again

come to walk in the peace in Christ that is

theirs.

Craig Snyder

Chapter 1

The Beginning

On October 24, 1971 something happened to me that I would never forget. After being a church member for fifteen years I believed Jesus Christ as my life. If you had asked me before this time if I was a Christian, I would have told you, "Well, of course I am. I am an American. I play church league softball, I am a church member, and I have been baptized." On that night all of this came to count for nothing in my life. I realized that I had not known Christ even though He knew me and had chosen me from before the foundation of the world.

I had attended a meeting sponsored by Campus Crusade for Christ, and the speaker was sharing how a religious leader named Nicodemus had come to Jesus at night. Jesus told this very religious man that he must be born again. He did not understand that, and neither did I. I just knew that I wanted out of that place. I now know that it was the power of the Holy Spirit that was at work in my life drawing me to Christ Himself. However, at that time I just wanted out. I was with a young lady who had invited me to the meeting. I thought that if I could get out of there and get her home, everything would be okay.

I did get her home, and I went home and went to bed. A friend was staying with me at the time and we were sharing a bedroom. About five o'clock in the morning I was still thinking about what I had heard. I cried out to Jesus and just said, "Save me Jesus." I did not know all the terminology; I just knew that I wanted Jesus. As soon as I cried out to Him, I was overcome with emotion. I did not know what was going on; I just knew something was happening. I tried to wake up my friend who was from Germany. In his thick accent, he said go back to sleep. That friend is now with Jesus face to face.

I went to the phone and called my closest boyhood friend who I always thought was a "real" Christian. He was different from the rest of us as a child and as a man. My friend had just been married, and his wife answered the phone just after 5a.m. She did not seem to be surprised at all when I said, "Pam, this is Craig. May I speak to Dan?" I told Dan what had happened, and he began to explain to me what was going on in my life. He did not seem surprised, he seemed very glad, in fact, excited. As he began to speak the truth of eternal life in Christ to me, I was overcome with peace.

I still did not understand it all, but in faith I did receive it all. I later realized that I had believed totally in Jesus and had received His life that He had given me from eternity past, as my life.

Morning came, and I was supposed to go over to my employer's house and rake leaves for his wife. I worked for the famous football coach, Wally Butts. Coach, as we called him, had been the head coach at the University of Georgia for twenty- two years. I traveled with him everyplace he went, and I drove his car. It was a great job as far as I was concerned. I did not have to do much. I had an expense account, a salary, a car provided, and best of all; I got to hang out with Coach. What a deal. People cared about what I said because I had been with Coach. He was great to me; he and his whole family treated me like family.

Well, getting back to leaf raking, I forgot to go. Sometime later in the morning Mrs. Butts called me and said, "Craig, where are you?" I look back and laugh at the answer I gave her and at her response to me. I said, "Mrs. Butts, I found God." She said okay and hung up. I realized that if you wanted to get out of leaf raking tell them that you found God. They can't get rid of you fast enough. I want to hasten to say that several years later after a lengthy illness, Mrs. Butts also trusted Christ. She was one of the nicest ladies that I ever knew.

For the next few days and weeks, all I wanted to do was read my Bible and talk about Jesus. I had called my friend, the girl that I could not wait to take home, and told her that I had trusted Christ. She was glad, and she also did not seem surprised. All these

Christians seemed to expect God to save people. She gave me a Bible that I began to read, and much to my surprise, I could understand it as I was reading it. Everything about me began to change. No one came to me and told me to start anything or stop anything. Things in my life did stop and things began to start, but no one told me to do anything. I did not know it then, but I am eternally grateful that they did not. I now know that my life had been exchanged with the life of Jesus Himself. The changes that were being made were the direct result of my having been given a new mind and a new heart. Things that I had wanted to do I no longer wanted to do, and things that I did not want to do, I now wanted to do. What a wonderful exchange this was.

OTHERS BEGAN TO SEE CHRIST IN ME

About a week after I received all that had been done and given me in Christ, my mother came into the room I was in and asked me, "Craig, what has happened to you?" She was crying as I told her that I had been saved. I did not know how to tell her. Sometimes, it is hardest to tell your own family. Isn't this sad? Well, I want to say that since that time, all my family has been saved, and all of them are walking with Christ in the power of His life. It is too wonderful to even describe.

My friends began to see a change in me also, and they began to ask questions. They did not have to ask much because I was telling them just as loud and often as I could about how good Jesus was. I wanted everyone that I loved and cared about to know the same Jesus that I knew. Some of them would make statements like, "I have read the Bible all the way through." That always surprised me because they went to the same places I did and did the same things I did. I don't know if they were believers or not, but I have come to know that being saved is not what you do, but what He did. I have decided to just love people and tell them what the God Head has done for them and given to them and encouraging them to believe it for themselves.

After I received and believed Christ, I was not as close to some of my friends as I had been in the past, and with many of them I have lost touch over the years. However, with many others I developed life long friendships, and they are more like family than friends. One example is my friend Gordon. Gordon was a very bright young man that I went to school with all the way through college. He was a great ball player, and I had played with him since I was twelve years old. He was in basic training in the Army Reserves stationed at Fort Dix, New Jersey, when he heard through some friends what had happened to me. He made the statement, "You know how Craig is, this will pass." I am glad to say that it did not pass. By the way, Gordon became a pastor. He also trusted Christ and went to seminary with me years later. That is a story for another time, though.

Having said all this let me say that Christ became my life. I was totally different. My life was truly transformed, and I was totally at peace. What a great way to live. He loved me, and I knew it, and I was falling in love with Him. This was the love relationship that I had always wanted. I had been very insecure in my life as I am sure many of you have been. For the first time, it did not matter what others thought of me or what I accomplished in business, sports, or life. I was in Christ, and He was in me. This is a great place to be, totally secure and dependent on Christ.

I was in the Army reserves at this time of my life, and one weekend a month we would have what we called drill. We would meet for two days and either go into the field or stay inside where we would do training. On one such weekend, we were on the back of a large army truck that was transporting us to the field for a weekend of camping and drills. Several of the guys on the truck with me were asking questions about a personal relationship with Jesus, and He was allowing me to answer their questions. It was not even something I worried about; He would just bring the answers to my mind and even many times scripture references. While this was going on, a young lawyer, who was not a believer, was trying to give me a hard time with ridicule and arguing. I did not mind; it was giving me a chance to share about my relationship with Christ without sounding preachy. This went on all the way to where we were going to have our weekend maneuvers.

This would seem inconsequential except that around two years later a man named Chris, who had become a close friend, came to me with a great revelation. He said that after hearing that lawyer try to tear me down in front of everyone on the truck and me not minding, he went home to his father who was a pastor and told him that he had seen a real Christian. Chris was in college and in a fraternity and realized that he had never been truly born again. He gave his life to Christ and was never the same. He also became a pastor in Atlanta. This is just one example of how Christ will use your life as you allow Him to live and walk in you. I did not know any other way to live than this, but I am sad to say that that was about to change.

I Met Religion

I want to start by saying that Campus Crusade for Christ had a profound impact on my life. It was through Campus Crusade that I heard the gospel of our Lord Jesus Christ. It was also through them that I developed skills that I still use in sharing the gospel. I am grateful for how they were used in my life and how they are being used around the world. They may be the largest sending organization of missionaries in the world. They were there for me when I was first saved, and I will always be thankful for how God used them in such a mighty way in my life.

I was also introduced to religion in a round about way at this time in my life. I don't blame anybody; it was something that just happened. I was asked if I wanted to attend a weekend conference with Campus Crusade for Christ at a nice hotel in Atlanta. I thought, a whole weekend to talk and learn about Jesus, count me in. The teaching was great and to this day is still a blessing in my life.

On Saturday morning I noticed everyone was sitting alone in the halls of the hotel and any other place where they could be alone. I asked the people what they were doing and they looked at me funny and said they were having a quiet time. I asked them, "What is that?" They looked at me really strangely then and told me that is when you read your Bible. I thought oh, ten o'clock that is when you read your Bible. I had been thinking that you read it whenever you want to read it.

It may seem a little ridiculous, but this did have a profound impact on my life. Very quickly, communing with God became something that I did, instead of an ongoing relationship with Jesus. Before this time, going to church was something I did because I wanted to do it. Reading my Bible was a desire in my life. I had stopped doing certain things because they were no longer the desire of my life, and I had started certain things because my wants had dramatically changed. In other words, Christ had totally changed me. I did not understand until later that this was not a change at all but an exchange. Christ had exchanged His life for my life. In the exchange, He had given me His mind, His heart and truly His desires.

Gradually, relationship was replaced with duty. I still went to church, but it became something that I should do. I attended Bible studies, and they became long. Other people around me were just like me. They had good motives; they were learning and teaching what we should and should not do. Although I still believed the Bible and still loved Jesus, the relationship was not the same. It seemed as if I was trying now to measure up to someone or something. I was now trying to do right instead of getting to know Him. What had happened? It was so gradual. It was not all at once, and no one ever said to me, stop desiring to be with Him and do these things. In many ways I did it to myself.

Self, that is a key word. I did not understand what the Bible says and teaches about self. I did not know that self, although it had died, still wanted to be in control. I did not know that self was, in fact, nothing more than that old term, flesh. I was now walking according to the flesh. I had been taught that flesh was lying, stealing, lust, anger and such. I did not know that there was such a thing as religious flesh, but I was beginning to experience it for myself.

I can tell you this, when the delight of knowing and being known by Jesus, the delight of walking in Him and with Him, turned into something that I should do rather than who I am, my delight in Him became my duty. Things were just not the same. Joy was gone, and I am afraid that for many people this is the life they know as a Christian. This was never the desire of

Christ for us. Our intimate love relationship with Christ was never to be out of duty. It is one of relationship. It is not my duty to love God with all my heart; it is my desire. If I told my wife, "Honey, I love you because it is my duty. I love you because I should," I doubt if she would be impressed. In fact, I can tell you that she would not be thrilled with our relationship at all.

Walking in Christ is not something that you do. If you are not careful, you will develop a plan of attack and say, "Okay I am going to do it. I am going to walk in Christ, no matter what." You would be making walking in Christ what you do instead of who you are. You are in Christ. He is your life. You don't try to have life; you just live it. Trust Christ to live His life through you. He will direct you; He will even give you a new heart's desire, a heart's desire that cannot be satisfied with anything less than total dependence on Him and a desire to know Him. He will reveal Himself to you and He will also reveal His will to you. He does this because He loves you and very deeply desires relationship with you.

Chapter 2

Abiding In Him

For years now, I have been writing letters to the Lord, and He sometimes uses my hand and writes personal letters back to me. I do believe that He communicates with me on a level deeper than even a soul level. I believe that He speaks on the spirit level. What He speaks on this deep personal level will never be contradictory to what scripture says. It can't be, or it is not from Him. It will, however, be very personal and very pointed as to what is going on in my life. I do believe that we should expect God to speak to someone He loves very much. This is really exciting because He loves me very much. He loves me unconditionally, and He will make His will known to me. It is His job to reveal Himself to me and to reveal His will to me. It is my job to listen and to obey which is to believe Him for what He says. Having said all that, I am going to share some of a letter between Jesus and me with you. It is personal, and I believe very practical, and if it applies to me, well, it probably applies to you, also.

A while back, I had been praying and desiring to have more of the joy of the Lord in my life. I did not realize that it was always available but it was not always appropriated. Here is the letter.

> Lord, abiding in You is my desire. It is key
> to everything in the Christian life, my life.
> Abiding in You is the only way that I can
> have the Father's joy.

What is abiding in You? I think that abiding in You is total dependence on You. Lord, I don't even know what that means, but I know that you don't want me to struggle or fear. If I am anxious or fearful, it is a tip-off that I am not enjoying the fruit of abiding in You.

You have said that I will bear much fruit. Bearing fruit is not a command; bearing fruit is a statement of fact. It is not up to me, it has already been decided. In John 15:16 it says, "You did not choose me, but I chose you and appointed you to go and bear fruit-- fruit that will last." You said that I have been chosen and appointed to bear fruit that will last. This is unbelievable, You chose me to bear fruit.

You have decided that You will cause me to bear fruit. The parts of me that keep me from bearing fruit are pruned and removed. Dead wood or wood that is taking up sap and not producing fruit is removed. It is for my good and has nothing to do with me.

Although pruning has nothing to do with me, I agree with the vinedresser, the Father, and ultimately it produces joy. I am so glad that it does produce joy. I am blessed by it, and it is for my good. I am so glad that it is nothing that I have to do in the flesh because I couldn't.

So, I guess I will go back to where I started, trusting You for everything. It is all You for my life. Always has been, always will be, this is abiding in You. It all goes back to faith. Believing is abiding in You. We abide by faith just like we were saved by grace through faith. We abide by grace through faith. Grace and faith are a gift of God, not anything we did that we should boast. Our boasting must be in You and Your faithfulness.

Abiding in You is as much a grace gift as salvation is. I can no more abide in my own power than I can be saved through my own power. If it is something that I think that I am doing to abide, then in fact I am not abiding at all. In other words, the more I strive, the less I abide.

Abiding will lead me to experience your love. Experiencing your love causes me to love others; this leads to your glory. Your glory causes others to want to know You. When they know You, it causes them to realize how much You love them. When they realize how much You love them, it causes them to love You.

Do you see what is happening here? It is a circle, a circle of life. It is all Him; we are in Him, chosen by Him, appointed by Him to abide in Him, to know Him and be loved by Him. What do we do? We receive and believe Him. Receive what and believe Him for what, for our life, our joy, our livelihood, for everything. I trust Him and receive His life in me. This allows Him to live His life in me. This produces His works in me. Wonderful works, works that are beyond anything that I could think up, let alone do.

All Him, well that is not a bad place to start. It is not a bad place to live. Abiding in Him is not just something that I do; it is who I am. I am in Him. I have no choice but to abide in Him. So, in other words, because of who I now am, I choose to abide in Him. It makes me want to say, "thank you Lord, your glory, your life, your joy, you have given them all to me."

When I started this book, I had to decide if I was going to be transparent with you or not. I had to decide if I was going to let you in on my desires, hurts, joys and sorrows. Well, I am going to let you in on my life. I believe as we realize that our life is hidden in Christ, and He lives His life through us, the walls will come down and our lives will become an open book. That does not mean that we will share everything that comes into our mind, but it does mean that we will be honest with God and with each other. We are who He has made us, and He has made us wonderfully.

I want you to realize that your abiding in Christ is not even up to you. The One who has chosen you holy, beloved, (Col. 3:12) from before the foundation of the world, (Eph. 1:4); is also the one who is faithful to complete what He has started. Again, I say; will you relax in Christ? This is not complacency; it is resting in Him. Believe that He will do what He says He will do. Believe that He has done what He said He has done.

In John 15:16, it says that we were chosen by God to bear fruit. It is His work and His alone. Our only work is to believe in Him, (John 6:29). Let me say it again, believe in Him, believe in Him, believe in Him. You can't even believe in Him in your own power. Believe, in the language of the Bible, means the same thing as faith. Faith is a gift of God; you don't work for it or earn it. You receive faith, His faith which is given to you. You can't conjure up faith; it is not magic. It is what the Bible says it is in Eph. 2:8,9; it is a gift.

It is silly for you to try to bear fruit. Bearing fruit is not something that you try to do. To bear means to carry. Don't you know that God never intended for you to carry anything? He will bear your burdens and your fruit. You are not to try to bear fruit; you will bear fruit because that is what you have been created to do. In Georgia we have many pecan trees. Each year in the fall something wonderful happens. Pecans that have been born on pecan trees fall off of them and they can be eaten. We put them in pies, we roast them, we put sugar on them, we dice them, we chop them and we put them in candy. There is no end to the ways we enjoy them. It is a natural thing for pecan trees to produce pecans. Do you know that the way many people can tell a pecan tree is that it is producing pecans? It is normal, and it is seasonal.

It would be foolish to go into a pecan orchard in the dead of winter and expect to find pecans. Pecan trees produce pecans in the proper season. God knows when the season of your life is. Pecan trees don't worry what season it is, they just go about the business of being pecan trees. Will you just go about the business of being who you are; one who was chosen of God, beloved, one who was chosen to produce fruit. All a pecan tree does is to abide. It abides in the soil in which it was planted and where all the nutriments are provided. It, in fact, does nothing but abide.

When the pecan tree is not producing the amount of fruit that it is capable of producing, a husbandman will come along and prune the tree and cut off the dead or diseased branches. He does this not because he is mad at the tree or because he is punishing the tree but because he is responsible for the tree and its condition. Also, he is responsible for the fruit.

Will you know that the Father is the husbandman, and He cares about you and He cares about your condition? He loves you, and he wants you to rest in Him. It is His job to produce fruit, and it is your job to abide. Don't try to do His job. James 4:10 says, "Humble yourself before the Lord, and He will exalt you". To humble yourself is to totally depend on God, believing in Him for everything in your life. The Bible says without faith it is impossible to please God. Trying does not please God, trusting Him, believing Him as your life, pleases Him.

Will you believe Him for every detail, every problem of your life, rest in Him, abide in Him, and depend on Him? This pleases Him and will cause you to bear much fruit. As you bear much fruit, your life will be filled with peace and joy. Others will see it and want it. They will receive Him and believe Him by grace through faith just like you did. The fruit you bear will cause others around you to bear fruit also.

There is one other thing that pecans do when they fall off of the tree during the fruit-bearing season. They fall into good soil and produce new pecan trees. They can bear one hundred-fold. They bear fruit, which leads to other trees being produced, and they also become fruit bearing trees. It is all part of the divine plan of the Father to produce much fruit, fruit that cannot be measured on this earth. It is up to Him, and He will make it happen.

Chapter 3

Overcome By His Love

Many years ago, a young college girl in my church asked me to speak at her educational psychology class at the University of Georgia. I had graduated from Georgia and was somewhat intimidated at the thought of going back there to speak. I did not know what I was going to speak on so when all else fails ask God to speak through you. That is what I did.

When I got to the class, it was a large class and all but two people in the class were young women. While I was looking at the class, after I had been introduced, I knew how God wanted me to begin. The first thing that I said was, "Today I am going to tell you what everyone here wants more than anything in the world." I had their attention; I am sure they were thinking,

"How does this man know what I want more than anything in the world?" I am also sure they were thinking that today was a day when there would be no lecture, and they would not have to take notes, in other words, a day off.

I told them what they desired more than anything was to be unconditionally loved. You should have seen the look on their faces. They looked vulnerable as if someone had discovered some deep secret that they had. They also looked like little girls that needed someone to hug them. I proceeded to tell them that there was someone who loved them unconditionally, and His name was Jesus. There were things that I still did not understand about the unconditional love of God for me. Why had I started my talk this way? Sometimes I had been in situations when God would totally redirect what I was going to say, and this was one of those times.

Over the years I have been involved with athletics and athletes and coaches. As a player, I always wanted to win, and I wanted to be surrounded with those I thought were winners. Much, if not all, of my self worth came from winning. Teams that I played on won, teams that I coached won. If I won, I felt good about myself, and if I lost, well, words won't describe how I felt. It was like a death. This carried over into the ministry with me. Churches that I pastored were all near the top in baptisms and giving and attendance. This was the case much of the time because I was so competitive that I wanted to be first in everything. I really wanted to see people trust Christ, but again I was getting my worth based on how I thought *my* church was doing. This led to much turbulence in my life.

As God was beginning to overcome me with His love, I began for the first time to realize that I didn't have to accomplish anything to have worth. I had worth because He had determined that I did. My children were athletes at the local high school and I had become close friends with the new football coach and athletic director. He was a Christian and asked me to be the Chaplin for the team. He and I would spend Fridays lining off the football field, eating lunch together and praying. I would go to practice and even get caught up in coaching the kids. I began to fall in love with these kids and they knew it.

Something very unusual happened with this group of young men; they began to change. Many of them, one by one, began to trust Christ, and it was more than, "thank you I see that hand." It was a change on the field, in the locker room, and in the classroom. The team had not been very good for a number of years; in fact, they had been one of the worst teams in Georgia. Georgia is one of the best states in the United States for high school football, and South Georgia is the best of the state. Maybe it is because there is not much to do in South Georgia but play sports and farm but for whatever reason it is huge in South Georgia.

I began to share with the guys that I loved them. They could see that their new coach loved them, and I told them that Jesus loved them even more than we did. They began to believe me. A large percentage of these young men did not know their fathers or did not have a father at home. I told them that because Jesus loved them, they could be the kind of fathers that they had always wanted. Every one of them related to this. I told them that in Christ, they were going to be godly husbands and fathers and they started to believe this.

As they began to experience unconditional love, for the first time for many of them, their attitudes and actions changed. We did not begin to win all at once, but our team was no longer the joke it had been. We went from one win to three the next year. Then from three wins to six the following year and then in the fourth year something took place that was extremely rare; champions were born.

This was our first senior class, and all they had ever known was love and acceptance. This did not mean that they were not disciplined. Discipline is one of the greatest forms of love, but it must be true godly discipline. The word discipline comes from the word to disciple. We become disciplers when we know Jesus. It is not just what we do; it is who we are. I began to share with them from James 4, that if they would humble themselves before the Lord, He would exalt them. I told them that according to the scriptures, the way we truly humble ourselves is to submit ourselves to Him, in other words, trust Him and believe Him.

That fourth season we had started with two wins and two games that we lost by a combined score of 67-0. We were a very anemic two and two; when in the fifth game, something happened. We were playing a team that was very good and one we really had no chance of beating, but win we did, 9-7. The team was the same, but for the first time the boys began to believe all that we were telling them. That team won nine games in a row and played for the state championship. We wound up winning twelve games that year and for the next two years we never won less than ten.

What had happened? Some say it was weight lifting, some say great coaching. Well, we had both of those things, and they were both great. But I firmly believe that for the first time I was around a group of boys that had been overcome by the love of God. They believed that we loved them, that God loved them, and they truly began to love each other. They became a real team. Egos were gone, there were no stars, and they were free to fail or succeed. They knew they were loved no matter what.

Race was not an issue on that team. In the locker room before games, we would spend time in prayer and sometimes singing. The guys would be laying all over each other, black and white. It was a beautiful sight, young men from different backgrounds and different races that were united in Christ. Our team was actually becoming one body. They were truly a team that loved each other.

There were more teams in the future with which I would have the pleasure of sharing the overwhelming, unconditional love of Christ. Not all became state champions or national champions, but many of the kids became champions of Christ. Why, because He loved them not based on what they had done but on what He had done for them.

As I was working with that first high school football team, I became a staff member with the Fellowship of Christian Athletes. I began working with 39 high school and college teams in South Central Georgia. I saw coaches and young people that were having their self-images determined by what others thought was success. If a coach wins, then others will think highly of him. If he does not win enough, whatever that is, then he has no worth as a coach and maybe in some people's eyes, even as a person. This is totally wrong. God determines worth, and He has determined that you have worth. Your worth is not based on anything that you do but totally on who He says that you are. Remember who you are; you will hear this a lot in this book; you are holy. You are totally and completely holy because He has declared you to be. Don't base your worth on what others say.

Others, many times are wrong. Don't be caught up in the world's way of measuring success. I can tell you this, many people others thought were a success and had it together were in fact afraid and discouraged. If you measure your life according to the flesh you will be miserable. Many people that the world called a success lived defeated lives and died broken men. How tragic this is, if they had only known that Jesus loved them just like they were.

Coaches, who understood their identity in Christ and were secure in who they were, could do something that other coaches could not. They could love unconditionally those who were under them, their players. They could give their players what they now had, freedom to fail. You may say, "freedom to fail, have you lost your mind?" No, I don't think so. You see, in everything that we do, failure is a big part of it. In athletics, like life, we fail more than we succeed. In baseball, if you bat 300 you are considered a success. What that means is that you are reaching base, having batted the ball safely, thirty percent of the time. That means that you failed seventy percent of the time. A seventy percent failure rate is acceptable in baseball, even considered good. This is freedom to fail.

Well, I want to go further, much further. Many people don't attempt things because they are afraid that they will fail or "mess up". They go through life not attempting things they would like to try. They fear what others will think of their failure and how they themselves will feel about their failure. The reason is because their image is shaped by what others think about them rather than what God thinks about them. They in fact fail because they don't attempt.

The goal of a coach is to train an athlete to perform at the highest level he is capable of performing. Not getting more out of him than he is capable of giving but getting all out of him that he is capable of giving. I have been around athletics all my life and I have seen many gifted athletes who did not give it their all. Why is this? I think I know. If an athlete gives his all and fails, then in his mind he considers himself a failure. But if he holds back, even subconsciously, he can say to himself, I could have done it if I wanted. People say, "he didn't want it bad enough". I think he did want it;

that is not the problem; that is the symptom. Many times, what appears to be, not wanting it bad enough, is in reality, fear of failure.

Okay, you may ask, what is the problem then? The problem is that people think their worth is based on what they do and not on who they are. When people know who they are in Christ, then whatever they attempt has no bearing on their identity. They are willing to give their all because success or failure will not change their self image. They know they are loved by Christ, and who they are in Him. Another way of saying this is that you will never be free to excel until you are free to fail. You will never be free to fail until you know you have been chosen by Him from before the foundation of the world and that He loves you unconditionally.

It is not enough for you to just know that you are born again. You must know that He loves you unconditionally, and that He is in the process of conforming you to His image. You must know that you are holy because He is holy, and you are in Him. You must know that you are righteous because He is righteous and you are in Him.

The next one is a biggie. You must know that you are forgiven of all of your sins, past present and future, because He has forgiven you at the cross. You aren't seeking forgiveness; you have been forgiven. This is a subject for another chapter but for now let's just say that you need to know that you are forgiven.

The greatest thing people need is to know that they are totally and completely loved by Christ. His love for them is not based on what they do, but on His character and His desire. He desired to love you; He proved it on the cross when He gave His life for you. Know this, Christ and God the Father and God the Holy Spirit love you. You are loved. Live your life as one who is loved. It will change everything about everything.

You can see that success is based on people knowing their identity in Christ and not based on what they do. You can even say that what you do will be determined by you knowing who you are in Christ. You must know who you are in Christ. If you don't know who you are in Christ then ask God to show you. As He does show you who you are in Him, tell others who they are in Christ. This is for everyone you lay your eyes on.

There is no one that He does not love and has given

His life to and for.

Chapter 4

Chosen by God

Everybody in one way or another is seeking happiness in life. Having been in the ministry for over forty years, I have counseled many people about many things. I can say that as a rule, Christians don't seem to be any happier than non-Christians. You may ask; why is this? Happiness can be a state of mind based on circumstances, and circumstances change often for the worse. The problem that can arise when our circumstances change is that we either will not know or we will not think on what we have been given in Christ and who we are in Him.

In this chapter we are going to examine some things about who we are and what we have been given in Christ. The first thing we are going to see is we are chosen by God. We are not chosen for a task as some would think, we are chosen for a position. The position for which we are chosen is holiness and beloved, Col. 3:12. The word holy means to be set apart. We have been chosen and set apart, not for a job or a task, but set apart to be loved. We get the word beloved from this, to be loved. Set apart to be loved by God. This is almost too good to be true, but it is true. He has chosen us just so He can love us. We were chosen so that He could do something for us, not so we could do something for Him. The very fact that we think that there is something that we could do for God shows that we don't have a complete understanding of who God is.

In Acts 17:24,25 the Bible says, "*The God who made the world and all things in it, since He is Lord of heaven and earth, does not dwell in temples made with hands;*

neither is He served by human hands, as though He

needed anything, since He Himself gives to all life and

breath and all things". God needs nothing from us; He

is complete in Himself. For us to think that God

created or chose us to do something for Him is totally

untrue. This is what got man in trouble in the garden

when he ate from the tree of the knowledge of good

and evil. The serpent told Eve that if she would eat of

the tree of the knowledge of good and evil, she would

be like God. What she forgot was that she was already

like God. She forgot who it was that God declared her

to be and so did Adam when Eve gave Adam the fruit

and he also ate.

The Bible tells us in the book of Genesis; Adam was

created in the image of God. God gave to Adam that

which He gave to no other part of His creation. He gave Adam His life. He actually breathed His life into Adam. You could say, Adam had I Am that I Am (YHWH) in him. Adam thought like YHWH because YHWH was his life. YHWH's way of thinking has always been right or one might say righteous.

Adam and Eve did not need to eat of the tree of the knowledge of good and evil to be like YHWH, they already were because He had chosen to give Himself to them. He had revealed Himself to them and they fellowshipped with Him as they were going. YHWH loved Adam and Eve unconditionally. His love was shown by the Triune God bringing them into their inner being at creation. It was pictured again with the restoration of fellowship by the shedding of innocent blood to make a covering for their nakedness. This was the first picture of the cross in the Bible.

Let's talk for a moment about unconditional love. My wife is a wonderful, gifted, beautiful, smart, talented woman. If you knew her, you would know what I said is true. If you don't know her you may be asking, "why would she ever marry you"? I am sure that many have asked that same question. I think I know the reason that a gifted concert violinist educated at Northwestern University in Chicago would give her life to someone like me. It was because she knew that she was loved unconditionally. Even though she has so much going for her, she, like so many others never felt unconditionally loved. When she finally did know that I loved her and that I would never leave her nor forsake her, she gave me her whole heart.

I do love her, I am committed to her, and I will never leave her. My love for my wife is not based on what she does for me. I sound a lot like Jesus; don't I? I am not Jesus of course, but I do have his mind. I do think like him. If my loving someone would give someone else the desire to trust me unconditionally, what do you think the unconditional love of God will do? He loves you, He loves me, He will never desert nor forsake you, Hebrews 13:5. This is the best news that there can be. He chose me, to love me, because He wanted to do it and He will never change His mind.

When we realize that the purpose of our being chosen by God is to be set apart and loved by Him, it changes everything. It certainly changes the way we think. Let me say it for you, "Jesus loves me". Many have sung about this all their lives but I don't think that it has really sunk in.

When my granddaughter was three years old, she may not have known many things but she knew that Papa loved her.   Because she knew that Papa loved her, it changed the way she thought about Papa. Papa was not someone to be served; he was someone who hugs her. When she saw Papa, she did not desire to be on her best behavior, she desired to run to him. Papa was not someone that she feared; he was someone that she loved. She loved him for one reason, because Papa loved her first. She was confident in the love that Papa had for her. Knowing her relationship with Papa influenced her actions. She had a desire to love Papa and to be with Papa. She wanted to do the things Papa did, not because she should but because it was now her desire. If Papa was washing the car she wanted to help. If Papa was picking up pinecones, she wanted to help. She wanted to be where Papa was and to do whatever Papa was doing. It was the desire of her heart to be with Papa and to be like Papa.

Will you know that Jesus loves you even in a greater way than I love my granddaughter? He desires to hug you, to have you run to Him. He doesn't want you to serve Him but for you to know Him, John 17:3. There will be work done but He is the one who will do it through you. It will be the desire of your heart and you will get to do things, because you want to do them, Psalm 37:3-4. Yes, Jesus loves me; this I know for the Bible tells me so.

When we come to know Christ and the love, He has for us, we will begin to love as we are loved. When we know Christ is our life, loving people becomes who we are and not what we do. As we begin to see people the way Jesus does, we begin to see people in a pitiful state, hurting, separated from God. We also see hurting people who don't know their position in Christ, and we are filled with compassion for them. We want to do something for them. We want them to know Christ and to know their position in Him.

This is the same compassion that Christ felt when he saw the pitiful sight in Matt 9:36-38; they were downcast like sheep without a shepherd. He wanted to do something about it and He did something. He died on a cross, rose from the dead and gave His life to them, so that they could come into this love relationship with Him. We can't do anything about people's pitiful state, but Jesus has done something. He has brought all men into Himself and given them the justification of life, Romans 5:18. It is now the desire of our heart to see people trust Him and know their identity in Him.

We must also know our identity in Him. When we come to know how much Christ loves us and who we are in Him, we want everyone, with whom we come in contact, to have this same understanding of his or her relationship with Christ.

The compassion, which we now have from Christ, leads us to have kindness, toward everyone, to those who love us and those who don't. Kindness is not what we now do; it is who we are. I have a friend that I admire very much. His name is Don. The thing that I admire so much about Don is that he is always so kind. This does not mean that Don is weak because he certainly is not weak. Don is a man's man. He is talented, handsome and athletic, but those are not the things that I think about when I am around Don. Don seems to care about people. He cares when they hurt and he is always building people up. It is not fake or flattery, it is who and how Don is. One day I said "Don you are always kind". What Don said back to me got my attention. He said, "Brother Craig, I think Christians ought to be kind; don't you?" Later I came to realize as did Don, that Christians are not kind because they ought to be but because it is who they are. It is not only Christ in me, but it is also me because I now think like Him. I have His mind. His life is now my life, in fact, He is my life, Colossians 3:4.

Because we know that it is all about what has been done for us, and what is being done through us, we know that it is not about us, but it is about Him. We know that we are dependent on Him and so we submit to Him. It is as you would say, all Him and none of me. He loves me and sets me apart to be loved by Him and I receive and believe Him.

Can you believe this? What a deal. Well, this is a picture of humility, I am in total need, and He meets that need, continually because He wants to do so. I receive what He has for me and believe Him for everything in my life. Humility is not saying that I am nothing. That can be false humility, which is pride. It is also a lie because Christ says that I am a pearl of great price. He says that I am fearfully and wonderfully made. No, humility is simply you submitting everything to God, depending totally on Him. It is drawing near to God and Him drawing near to you, James 4:7,8. Humility is not what we do. It is a way of life. I know that without Christ I have no hope but that He Himself is now my hope. He is my life.

As I receive and believe Him, I receive His compassion and kindness, and humility, and they become mine. I become gentle in spirit. Gentle does not mean weak. Gentle is power under control. I don't have to fret or confront. I know the source and I know the power; gentle spirits are not afraid. They are patient, knowing that the one with all power is in control and that He loves me. In other words, He is in control. When I strive to be in control, I find that fear dominates my life. Usually it is fear of failure of some sort.

Part of the fruit of the Spirit is patience. When I try to be in control patience is something that is lacking in my life. Patience and fear can't co-exist. When we know that our dear Jesus is faithful, fear is gone and we trust Him. Trusting Him is a synonym for patience. We are willing to wait on Him because He knows what is best.

Have you ever noticed that when something seems out of your control or out of your comfort zone that you are afraid? It may be over health, finances, family problems or anything. I know this; it is always something that you can't control. What seems to be the problem is not the problem at all, but it is the symptom of the problem. The problem is that you don't believe that God is able or that He cares. Rather than address the fear, address the problem. Know that

God does care and that He knows what is going on and that He will allow nothing to come into your life that will not benefit you because He loves you. In other words, believe that God is in control, and He loves you and He cares.

As we are willing to trust God with our own lives, we become willing to trust Him with the lives of others, for the lives of those we love. We trust Him to do what we can't. We want to bear others burdens, Colossians 3:13. We hurt when they hurt just as we will rejoice with them when they rejoice. This is like Christ. He hurts with us and rejoices with us. But unlike us, He is not only able to empathize; He is able to solve problems. We can't but He will. We must continue to trust Him with the lives of others; after all, the way we have been dealing with the lives of others isn't working anyway.

Bearing with one another will lead people who know their identity in Christ to begin to forgive others. This will become who we are and not what we do. Forgiveness according to the flesh is based on what others do. If they say they are sorry, *and really mean it,* we will forgive them. If they don't really mean it, we won't forgive them. This is not of Christ. In Christ, we will forgive because we are set apart and are being loved by God and we are forgiven by God. Sometimes people have a hard time forgiving because they don't believe that they are fully forgiven.

In Ephesians 4:32 it says, "*And be kind to one another, tenderhearted, forgiving each other, just as God in*

Christ also has forgiven you". In Colossians 2:13 it says, *"When you were dead in your transgressions and the uncircumcision of your flesh, He made you alive together with Him, having forgiven us all our transgressions".* In verse 14 it goes on to say, *"Having canceled out the certificate of debt consisting of decrees against us, which was hostile to us; and He has taken it out of the way, having nailed it to the cross".* Can you believe this? While you were dead in your transgressions, He made you alive together with Him. The Word goes on to say, having forgiven us all our transgressions. The Word says all our transgressions.

Let me ask you a question; what does all leave out? You have been forgiven all, or you have not been forgiven at all. The tense of the word used in the Greek for forgiven in Colossians 2:13 is aorist and the voice is middle. You may be saying so what. Well, as we say in South Georgia, I am going to tell you so what. This word, forgiven, means completed action. Not only does it not need to be done again, it can't be done again. He forgave us and He chose us. Our part is to believe Him. Believing Him is critical, but with His mind that He gives us, we will believe Him.

Will you believe what He says about you? Will you believe that you are forgiven? He said that you are. The voice of the verb forgive is middle voice. This is also very exciting. This verse could be translated, having forgiven us, because he wanted to forgive us. Do you understand what this verse has stated? God the Father and Christ the Son, while we were yet sinners, have together as an act of their own will, chosen to forgive us once and for all, because they wanted to forgive us. You can't understand this with the natural mind.

He took care of this problem also. He gave us His mind and His heart. Nothing like this exist outside of Christ. Outside of Christ, forgiveness is conditional, based totally on what another person does. If people don't say they are sorry, and "really mean it", then we won't forgive them. This leads to a bitter spirit and will be like sand in machinery to the life of the Christian. No, the Christian must and will forgive, even before the offense. Forgiveness is part of Christ' life, and after all, that is whose life we have.

Don't be discouraged and say you can't do any of these things, of course you can't. That is what makes it so special; He does it all through you. All of this is because you are forgiven; you don't do anything to get forgiveness. Please know this one thing, you are forgiven. Live like you are forgiven. If you do, there will be a great desire to forgive others, it is who you are. You are in Christ, you are forgiven and you forgive.

None of this will take place without us knowing that we are loved. So, know this, you are loved, with perfect love, God's unconditional love. Because of this, wear it; let everyone see your new outfit. You are clothed in and with God's love. Wear it proudly. This love you are wearing is what everyone wants. It is the perfect bond of unity that holds us together.

Let me say it another way, the love that you wear is the glue that holds the family together. It is not what families do for one another that hold them together. What they do for one another is brought about because of the fact that they are all wearing God's love. Even those who don't know and wear God's love will be influenced by God's love. His love is shown in His Word, and it never returns void. His Word is Christ. Love, God's love, is a picture of Him, and it certainly never will return void. Wear it proudly, confidently, and humbly, knowing that it is a good and perfect gift from God.

Several years ago, I was in Argentina. While I was there, I saw a yellow dress that I thought would look very pretty on my granddaughter. It was December and in Argentina that is springtime and the weather was warm and sunny. Back in Georgia it was cold and rainy. When I returned home and gave the dress to my granddaughter, she looked forward to wearing the dress but had to wait until springtime in Georgia. When she finally did wear the dress, it made her feel special. She felt so good in the dress that everyone who saw her bright smile and radiant spirit also felt good. You might say that what she was wearing changed the way people around her felt. Their minds for a moment were off their own troubles and fears and they were feeling good about a little girl who was wearing a pretty yellow dress. This is just like you wearing God's love. Wearing God's love will change the way you see yourself and the way you see yourself will have an impact on those around you.

Wearing the love of God, from the inside, being patient, kind, compassionate, humble, and forgiving will truly lead to unity, Colossians 3:14. This is the only way there will be real unity; when we are all part of one body. Only Christ can make us one body, this is a picture of the body of Christ. The body of Christ comes from Christ who is the bridegroom, taking His bride, marrying her and the two becoming one. We have in fact been married to Christ and we are now one with Him. We are the bride of Christ. We are not only His bride, but we are now the children of God the Father, just as Christ is the Son of God. That makes us brothers to others that are the children of God.

When we know our position and calling, we will have the peace of God ruling in our hearts, Colossians 3:15. We will realize that we all were called individually to be part of the body of Christ and we will have a thankful spirit. We will be thankful, not because we think that we should be or because we have been commanded to be; but because it is who we are and how we are.

God not only gives us a thankful spirit but He also gives us His mind, the mind of Christ. Because we have the mind of Christ and His peace and a thankful heart, our desire will be for Him and His Word. His Word will dwell in us because He dwells in us. God's Word, as it dwells in us energized by the Holy Spirit, will lead to His wisdom dwelling in us.

As His wisdom lives in us, we will teach and admonish with His wisdom. Again, it will not be us doing it according to the flesh, but it will be the Word Himself, (YHWH), teaching and admonishing the only way He can, with true Godly wisdom. All wisdom comes from the Lord. If it is not from the Lord, it is not wisdom; it is foolishness. To man, the wisdom of God may seem like foolishness, but still the living Word is who transforms men's lives. So, don't worry about what you think man will say. Let Christ live out His life through you and watch others be amazed at the wisdom that you now posses.

As God gives you His wisdom, you will begin to teach and admonish one another with psalms, hymns and spiritual songs, Colossians 3:16. These will flow out of you because they are part of you. Your singing will lead to a thankful heart, and a thankful heart will lead to your singing. If you have a hard time singing God's hymns, psalms and spiritual songs you need to examine your heart and see if it is thankful. When you realize how much you are loved and forgiven, and who loves you, you will be thankful.

God tells us through Paul in Colossians 3:17 that, *"whatever we do in word or deed, do all in the name of the Lord Jesus, giving thanks through Him to God the Father"*. Again, some of you are now thinking that you must start or stop something; you can't! You are dead to the flesh. The flesh can't produce anything that pleases God or brings Him glory.

Stop *trying* to praise or give thanks to Him in word or deed. The Bible says here that we are to give thanks *through Him*. Thanksgiving is even done by Christ through us. He gives us new hearts, thankful hearts to God the Father, through Him. Even thanksgiving is a grace gift. When you know your identity and position in Christ, thanksgiving will flow out of you because you are truly thankful, it is who you are.

Chapter 5

Discovering The Blessings Of God Through Troubles

Sometimes we fall into the trap of thinking that the blessings of God are based on what we do. Sometimes we think it is our job to find God and to find His will. This could not be further from the truth. It is God's job to reveal Himself to us. He will always do His job.

You are not a better parent than God. Even when your children don't have a clue as to what they should do, because you love them, you reveal your will to them. One of the reasons that people toil in trying to find the will of God is because they don't understand how much God really loves them. The will of God is something He reveals to us because He loves us unconditionally and desires to bless us

In this chapter we are going to see three things about God and the way He reveals Himself to us. He reveals Himself to us in ways we may not expect. He reveals to us things we may not expect. And finally, He reveals His will to us at times we may not expect.

In Genesis 28:10 -22, Jacob had just stolen Esau's birthright. The birthright was the blessing that was given to the oldest son. The birthright was due Esau, the older brother, but it was given to Jacob fraudulently. Jacob is now fleeing to Laban, Rachel's brother. Jacob comes from a long line of deceivers. Abraham and Isaac were both righteous men, but their righteousness was not based on what they did. Their righteousness was a gift of God. On more than one occasion, both of these men gave their wives away because they were afraid. They were both cowards and liars, but in spite of this God called them righteous.

We see that righteousness is a gift of God and not

based on the actions of man.

> Genesis 28:10-22:
> *10Then Jacob departed from Beersheba and went toward Haran.*
> *11 And he came to a certain place and spent the night there, because the sun had set; and he took one of the stones of the place and put it under his head, and lay down in that place.*
> *12 And he had a dream, and behold, a ladder was set on the earth with its top reaching to heaven; and behold, the angels of God were ascending and descending on it.*
> *13 And behold, the LORD stood above it and said, "I am the LORD, the God of your father Abraham and the God of Isaac; the land on which you lie, I will give it to you and to your descendants.*
> *14 "Your descendants shall also be like the dust of the earth, and you shall spread out to the west and to the east and to the north and to the south; and in you and in your descendants shall all the families of the earth be blessed.*
> *15 "And behold, I am with you, and will keep you wherever you go, and will bring you back to this land; for I will not leave you until I have done what I have promised you."*

*16 Then Jacob awoke from his sleep and said,
"Surely the LORD is in this place, and I did not
know it."*

*17 And he was afraid and said, "How awesome is
this place! This is none other than the house of
God, and this is the gate of heaven."*

*18 So Jacob rose early in the morning, and took
the stone that he had put under his head and set
it up as a pillar, and poured oil on its top.*

*19 And he called the name of that place Bethel;
however, previously the name of the city had
been Luz.*

*20 Then Jacob made a vow, saying, "If God will
be with me and will keep me on this journey that
I take, and will give me food to eat and garments
to wear,*

*21 and I return to my father's house in safety,
then the LORD will be my God.*

*22 "And this stone, which I have set up as a
pillar, will be God's house; and of all that Thou
dost give me I will surely give a tenth to Thee."*

In Genesis 28:10-22 we see how God reveals himself to

us in ways we may not expect. We see that Jacob is

running from Esau. Jacob was wise in the world's eyes

to run from Esau. Esau was a hunter and

outdoorsman. Jacob would have been considered a

mama's boy. Esau was Isaac's favorite son; he was the kind of son that every father wanted. He was strong, able to provide, able to lead and defend. Jacob unlike Esau was his mother's favorite. He was not someone who loved the outdoors or was considered a man's man. Most of us have known people just like Jacob and Esau, and most of us would choose one we liked better than the other.

In Jacob's mind, he did not measure up to what he thought his father wanted. There are many people today who don't measure up, in their own mind, to what they feel others think of them. The problem is not what others think, but the problem sometimes is what they think others think. As a result of this, they spend a great deal of time running and hiding.

Whether they measure up or not is not the problem, the problem is, they don't think they measure up.

I want you to hear this: in Jesus you do measure up. You are in Christ; and He is in you. Why do you want to be measured by things that are going to perish? Don't you know that you have been created in the image of God? Jesus himself has measured you, and you have been found righteous. You are in the process of being conformed to His image; He is not finished yet, but He sees you now as complete. Whom are you going to believe? Are you going to believe the world and its false standards, or are you going to believe what the Word of God says? The Word of God says you are holy and you are righteous. You are loved by God and are seated with Christ on His throne. If you are seated on a throne, then that makes you royalty.

You are as much royalty as Christ because He is in you and you are in Him. When you finally realize this truth, it will change the way you think about everything.

Well, getting back to Jacob running from Esau, he goes through Bethel. When it comes time for Jacob to rest for the night, he puts a rock under his head, uses it for a pillow, and goes to sleep. That night YHWH spoke to Jacob in a dream. He had never spoken to Jacob before. Up until this time Jacob referred to YHWH as the God of Abraham and Isaac but never his own God. We can see that YHWH was seeking Jacob and Jacob was not seeking YHWH. This is the same way Jesus sought you. He twice said in John chapter six, "no one can come to me unless the Father who sent me draws him".

It is important to understand who YHWH is. YHWH spoke to Moses at the burning bush, and He told him his name. He referred to himself in the English as, I Am that I Am. The Hebrew word for I am is YHWH. The one who is speaking to Jacob is the same one who spoke to Moses. He is the same one who spoke to Abram before He changed his name to Abraham, and He is the same one who spoke to Isaac. In the New Testament Jesus said in John 8: 58, "before Abraham was born, I Am". The Jews who heard this picked up stones to throw at Him, not because they didn't understand what he was saying but because they did understand. They understood Him to be saying that He was God. That is exactly what He was saying. He was claiming to be the God of the Old Testament, YHWH Himself.

YHWH was seeking Jacob in the Old Testament to pour out His blessings on him. Jesus seeks you. Let me say that again, Jesus seeks you. You may think you are the one seeking Him, but He is the one seeking you. Why would He do this? He does it because He wants to do it. Jesus said in the Bible that He came to seek and to save that which was lost. You are no longer lost. Does He stop seeking you because you're no longer lost? No, He loves you. He reveals himself to you; He desires your company, and He wants to bless you. He literally seeks you out to bless and love you.

There is a major point here; it is all about Him and not about us. His blessing toward us is not based on us but on Him. I want to state again, Colossians 3:12 says, we are chosen by God, holy and beloved. God chose to set us apart and love us because He wanted to. It is all based on Him and His desire.

We're going to look at a second truth from Genesis 28: 13. God reveals to us what we do not expect. YHWH told Jacob in verse 13, "The land on which you lie, I will give you and your descendants". This is the last thing Jacob would have expected. He had just stolen his brother's blessing. His father was mad at him, and his brother was mad at him. His brother was mad enough to kill him. He expected judgment; he did not expect a blessing.

Do you expect a blessing from God today, or do you live your life thinking that God is going to get you?

This is just like God; when we deserve judgment, He chooses to bless us. We were sinners deserving judgment. But on the cross, He who knew no sin became sin so that we might become the righteousness of God, 2nd Corinthians 5:21. He became sin and gave us His position, a righteous son. There is no explaining this according to the world. In the world's eye, those that deserve judgment get judgment. I'm glad that Christ is not like the world. He declared me righteous and I believed Him. It was based solely on Him and has nothing to do with my actions.

Back to Jacob, he was expecting judgment but instead he was given land for which he had not worked. The blessings of God are not based on what we do for Him. If you were seeking someone to bless, it would not have been Jacob, but God did. He chose to bless Jacob before he was born.

Romans 9: 10-13,

And not only this, but there was Rebekah also, when she had conceived twins by one man, our father Isaac; for though the twins were not yet born, and had not done anything good or bad, in order that God's purpose according to His choice might stand, not because of works, but because of Him who calls, it was said to her, "The older will serve the younger." Just as it is written, "Jacob I loved, but Esau I hated."

This does not mean that God did not also love Esau. Esau was able to look out for himself and he did, he was an independent person, needing no one. I think YHWH detest independent living, depending on self because of what it does to us. We see later that God did in fact bless Esau greatly.

I don't pretend to understand why God chose to bless Jacob; I just know that He did. It had nothing to do with Jacob, and it had everything to do with God.

Once you know your identity based on whom God has made you and how He has blessed you, your actions will change. We want people to act a certain way in order to be blessed. God blesses and then actions follow. Again, He gives us His righteousness and His Holiness and loves us and then gives us His position. He gives us His life, and then we begin to live like who we now are. Who are we? We are someone who has the righteousness of Jesus, the holiness of Jesus, who is loved by Jesus, and has the very life of Jesus. No matter how you feel, this is who you are, based on what He did and gave. Knowing to whom you belong and who you are will change the way you think about yourself. A dear friend of mine once told me, when he was a child, he had learning difficulties. He had no self-confidence about anything. He had no father and a mother that was only proud of him when he excelled in athletics. He had been labeled and placed in learning disabled classes in school. One day a teacher came to him and said, "you need to stop hanging around those bad boys and stay with the good boys where you belong". To you or me, this would not have seemed like a very big deal, but to him it was huge. Someone he respected had called him good and told him that he belonged with those that were good. My friend told me that this was a turning point in his life. He was soon placed in regular classes in school and even went on to graduate from college. He became an All-American football player and even played in the NFL. He is now ministering the grace of our Lord Jesus Christ to young people in an athletic based ministry. This turnaround took place because a caring teacher told a little boy that he belonged with the good boys and he believed her. He not only believed who the teacher said he was, he later believed who Jesus said He was. Remember this, our words matter. Tell people who they are and what Jesus has done and given. Jesus cares about you and he tells you that you are righteous and holy, and you belong to Him. Will you believe Him? Believe that you are who God says you are and watch your life change.

Not only did YHWH bless Jacob with land, He gave him the same promise that he gave his grandfather Abraham. He told Jacob in Genesis 28:14 that his descendants would be like the dust of the earth. I believe he was talking about a physical blessing for many Jews born of the flesh. I believe he was also speaking of a spiritual blessing for those He loved, "For

God so loved the world....". YHWH gave this promise to Abram before Abram knew Him. YHWH is now giving this promise to Jacob before Jacob knows Him. Jacob had referred to YHWH as the God of Abraham and Isaac. Jacob did not refer to YHWH as his God.

YHWH also told Jacob in Genesis 28:14, that in his descendants all the families of the earth would be blessed. The world has been blessed by the Jews in many ways, through medicine, culture, government, hygiene and most of all through the Lord Jesus Christ. The Jews were to take the message of faith in YHWH to the world.

YHWH also made a promise to Jacob in Genesis 28:15 on that fateful night in Bethel, when He said, "I am with you". Not I will be with you, not I was with you, but I am with you. What a great promise YHWH made to Jacob!

This promise is not based on what Jacob had done for YHWH. Jacob had done nothing for YHWH. This promise is not based on a specific area. In verse 15 YHWH said, "I will keep you wherever you go". This promise in Christ is also yours. He will keep you no matter where you go, no matter what. This is not based on what you do, but on what He says.

The promise to Jacob is not based on time. In verse 15 YHWH also said, "I will not leave you until I have done what I have promised". This promise will not be over until all his descendants are brought into the promise. He will keep His promise of not leaving for eternity.

Jacob's name was soon to be changed to Israel. Israel was the father of 12 sons. Of those sons Jesus was born from the line of Judah. The promise that YHWH made to Jacob and his descendants is now ours

because we are in Christ. We were grafted into the

family of the Jews through Christ. We are adopted as

sons according to the Bible.

*Romans 8:15 "For you have not received a spirit of
slavery leading to fear again, but you have received a
spirit of adoption as sons by which we cry out, "Abba!
Father!"*

Ephesians 1:4-5 says, *"just as He chose us in Him before
the foundation of the world, that we should be holy and
blameless before Him. In love He predestined us to
adoption as sons through Jesus Christ to Himself,
according to the kind intention of His will."* All the
blessings are now ours based on the work of another.

The last thing we are going to look at in this chapter is

YHWH reveals His will to us at times we may not expect.

Jacob did not doubt that YHWH existed. He knew YHWH

existed. His father knew YHWH and he spoke of Him

often. Jacob's grandfather, Abraham, also knew YHWH.

Jacob's problem was not that he did not know about

YHWH, he knew about YHWH. Jacob's problem was that he did not know YHWH personally.

The last thing Jacob expected was for YHWH to visit him while he was fleeing. He had sinned against Isaac, and he had sinned against Esau. He was tired; he was broken, and he was sleeping on a rock alone in the desert. That is when YHWH chose to reveal Himself to Jacob. When all hope was lost and when his life, as he had known it, seemed over, YHWH blessed Jacob.

Is this not a time, no matter what's going on in your life, Jesus would reveal himself to you? Is this not a time, that you would know the promise of His life, eternal life as your life? When all seems hopeless, God Himself is getting ready to bless you!

Chapter 6

Only Believe

Over the years I have met many well-intentioned people that have a great desire to work for Jesus. They wanted to do something for Him. These people had right motives, but right motives don't necessarily lead to what is of Christ. They were no different than people I have also known who used to say, "Do something even if it's wrong". It may sound appropriate to just do something, but when you do something that you have to undo, you are really backing up. You are not helping a situation; you are in fact hindering the situation. In the world, when you don't know what to do, what you should do is nothing. It goes against the grain of the flesh to just do nothing. If you feel that you must do something for Christ, then you are operating according to the flesh. As you are walking in the Spirit, when you don't know what to do, you do nothing. Another way of saying this is, "when you don't know what to do, wait on God".

In this chapter we are going to look at what it means to believe in Christ and how that believing in Him will lead to what we ultimately do. I know this; all that we do, when we are living by faith in Him, will be done with His power. When we live a life of total dependence on Him and believe Him for everything in our lives, our yoke is easy and our load is light. More than we could ever imagine will get accomplished and it won't burn us out.

In John chapter 3, we look at a man named Nicodemus. Nicodemus was a leader of the Jews, and He came to Jesus at night. I have heard many explanations as to why he chose not to come to Jesus in the day. Some say that he did not want to be discovered with Jesus. Others say, the crowds were too large to get to Jesus in the daytime. The Bible does not tell us why Nicodemus came to Jesus at night, so I won't either. The Bible does say that Nicodemus was a man of the Pharisees. It refers to him as a ruler of the Jews. We don't know for sure that Nicodemus was a member of the Sanhedrin but there is a good chance that he was. In John 3:10, Jesus referred to Nicodemus as *"the teacher of Israel"*. He did not say; you are a teacher of Israel. He referred to him as the teacher of Israel. Nicodemus, according to Jesus, was at the very least, influential among the Jews. Jesus said to Nicodemus, "Are you the teacher of Israel and do not understand these things?"

When Nicodemus came to Jesus, he said to Him, "Rabbi, we know that you have come from God as a teacher; for no one can do the signs that you do unless God is with him." Nicodemus did not know what to say to Jesus or even what to call Him; he just knew he wanted to know what was going on with Jesus. Nicodemus was not saying that Jesus was God but that God was with him. There is a big difference. Either Jesus is who He claimed to be, YHWH, or He is a liar. He can't just be a great teacher. Jesus, being fully God as well as fully man, was able to look into Nicodemus' heart and know his real need. Jesus told Nicodemus, "Truly, truly, I say to you, unless one is born again, he cannot see the kingdom of God." Nicodemus did not understand what Jesus was saying, but in his mind, he wanted to do something. Nicodemus asked Jesus, "Can a man become small again and enter a second time into his mother's womb?" Jesus answered, "Truly, truly I say to you, unless one is born of water and spirit he cannot enter into the kingdom of God." Jesus had told him unless one is born again, he wouldn't see the kingdom of God. Now He was telling him, unless one is born of water and spirit he will not enter into the kingdom of God. To a Pharisee like Nicodemus, this must have been very frustrating. Going into the kingdom of God was totally out of his hands. A Pharisee was adept at keeping the law or so he thought, and now Jesus is telling Him he would not see or enter the kingdom of God unless he is born again. Nicodemus knew one thing; no one controlled his own birth.

What does it mean to be born of water and spirit? I'm a man, and I have never given birth to a baby. I was, however, with my wife when our four children were born. Before each child was born, my wife's water broke. A water birth, I believe, is a physical birth. We might call this a natural birth. Nicodemus understood a natural birth. He was wise in all the ways of Israel. Israel was practicing modern medicine long before the rest of the world. They understood things, based on the word of God in the Old Testament that the rest of the world is just beginning to understand. Nicodemus understood a natural water birth. He also thought, like other wise men of his day, with his natural mind and did not understand spiritual things.

The things that Nicodemus did not understand and could not understand were the things that required the mind of Christ. Jesus told him, "You must be born of the Spirit." When you are born of the Spirit, you are born again. You have a new mind, a new heart, a new way of thinking. You now think with your new mind and your new heart because you have the heart and mind of Christ. You think like Him. Jesus told Nicodemus, unless you are born again you will not see, you will not enter, you will not even understand the kingdom of God. There is a word for thinking different; it is repentance. God changes the way you think totally. When you are born again, you can never sin again as a way of life because you think like Him. With your new heart you will have a terrible distaste for sin.

What Nicodemus needed was a heart transplant. He needed a new heart but not just any heart. It had to be the right blood type and it had to be the perfect heart for him if he were going to enter the kingdom of heaven. There was only one heart that would do. There was only one blood type that would work also. The blood type that was required was type S. S stands for sinless. The sinless blood of Jesus was the only blood that would work for this transplant to be successful. The new heart that is given is none other than the heart of Jesus. The good news is that He has given His life and heart to everyone from the cross which is eternal. To benefit from this eternal action by Christ for all men, one must believe what He has already done on their behalf. Not only does He give His heart and blood to everyone, but as one believes Him, He also gives a new mind, a totally new way of thinking. We now have the mind of Christ; we think like Him.

Today, I am sad to say, there are those who have the mind of Christ but they are thinking according to the flesh. They are thinking as if they don't have the mind of Christ. The Bible says; they are walking according to the flesh. They are not of the flesh, but they are walking and thinking as if they are of the flesh. How tragic this is in the life of the believer.

Let's continue looking at John chapter 3 as Jesus shares with Nicodemus. Jesus is going to meet Nicodemus where he is and share with him what He wants for him. Jesus told Nicodemus in John 3:14, "As Moses lifted up the serpent in the wilderness, even so must the son of man be lifted up." Nicodemus, being the teacher of the Jews, knew this was referring to Numbers 21. When the fiery serpents bit the children of Israel while they were in the desert with Moses; if they would believe and look toward the serpent that had been lifted up in the midst of the camp, they would be healed and live. If they did not do this, they would die. This involved faith on the part of those who had been bitten. Another way of saying this is, unless they believed, they would die.

Had the serpent already been lifted up in the wilderness? The answer is yes. Did they need to believe it and look to it? Again, the answer is yes. Today men live as if they are dead without hope, when in fact Jesus has been lifted up on their behalf. John 3:15 says, "So that whoever believes will in Him have eternal life." Eternal life is "in Him". It is not in a thing or an action; eternal life is in a person, Jesus. In John 3:16, it says the same thing. It also says the reason we have eternal life, is because He loves us.

The idea, which is the same in both verses, is that believing in Him leads to knowing and experiencing eternal life. Not just believing, but believing in Him. Today people want to believe in many things other than only Jesus. Acts 4:12 said, "*And there is salvation in no one else; for there is no other name under heaven that has been given among men by which we must be saved.*"

We must examine a few things here. First of all, what is eternal life? Jesus gives us the definition of eternal life. While praying for his disciples in John 17:3, Jesus said, "this is eternal life; that they may know You, the only true God and Jesus Christ whom You have sent." By Jesus' own definition, eternal life is knowing God the Father and Christ the Son.

If knowing God the Father

eternal life, then how can we kn Son is

Christ the Son? The only way we can ather and

Father and Christ the Son is by believing inhe

Another way of saying this is when we believe in

we come to know the justification of life, His life,

which was given to all men through one act of

righteousness, Romans 5:18. The word that is

translated believe from the Greek in the New

Testament is *pistuo.* This is the same word that is

translated faith. The word faith and believe in the New

Testament are inter-changeable. Believing equals faith.

Gal. 2:16 Knowing that a man is not justified by the works of the law, but by the faith of Jesus Christ, even we have believed in Jesus Christ, that we might be justified by the faith of Christ, and not by the works of the law: for by the works of the law shall no flesh be justified. (King James) ɔur behalf is what justifies. One

The faith o ..d was enough and begins to know

believes ..t was given, His life Rom. 5:18, His

and wal, while we were enemies, Rom. 5:10. You

recofat you were made alive while you were dead,

bel;. You know and believe all this which is eternal

F

., His life freely given to all men.

There is a problem for those who want to just do something; you cannot even believe in your own power. Believing is a grace gift. The Bible says in Ephesians 2: 8, 9, *"For by grace you have been saved through faith; and that not of yourselves it is the gift of God; not as a result of works so that no one may boast."* It has been wrongly preached that grace is God's part and faith is man's part, and when the two come together salvation takes place. This preaches fine, it is just wrong. The Bible clearly says that grace and faith go together; they are both gifts of God. They are not the result of work

so that no one can boast. If your faith was a result of

something you did, you could boast. However, the

Bible says, it is not the result of works. You did

nothing but receive God's grace and God's faith. It is

not about you, it is about Him.

Jesus said in John 1:12, "*But as many as received Him,*

to them He gave the right to become children of God,

even to those who believe in His name." Let me say it

another way, when you receive Him and believe in His

name, you **know** you are God's child. Remember,

eternal life is knowing the Father and the Son whom He

sent. Jesus said twice in John chapter 6, "No one can

come to Me unless the Father who sent Me draws him."

I am not trying to say anything other than what I've

already said; eternal life is a gift of God. Left alone no one would believe. Even believing is a gift of God. Continuing with John 3:17; Jesus told Nicodemus that God did not send His Son into the world to judge the world, but that the world might be saved through Him. He goes on to say that he who believes in Him is not judged. But he who does not believe is judged already because he has not believed in the name of the only begotten son of God. What is the name of the only begotten son of God? According to Jesus Himself the name is YHWH. In John 8:58, Jesus said, "Before Abraham was born, I Am." Jesus claimed to be I Am. He claimed to be I Am, the one who spoke to Moses at the burning bush, because that is who He was and is. Hebrews 13:8 says, "*Jesus Christ is the same yesterday and today, yes and forever.*" Believing in Jesus, leads one to know Him and His eternal life in Him. Do you understand this? You are not judged anymore, not by

the Father, not by the Holy Spirit, not by Jesus and

certainly not by anyone else. When you trusted Christ,

you judged yourself as guilty, deserving of death, but

Christ has judged you righteous and holy based on

what He did. Believe what He says about you. It is true

from before the foundation of the world when He

chose you, Eph. 1:4.

An after thought on this subject of judging is don't do

it. If the Father turned the job of judging over to the

Son, Jesus, and He did not come to judge, then why do

we think that it is our job to judge people? What we

should do is pray that people would come to know

Jesus in a personal way, the way He and the Father

know each other. This is true because they have

brought you into relationship with themselves because

they wanted to from eternity past. Believe Him that it is true.

I believe the Bible teaches that Nicodemus was an honest seeker. There were however other Pharisees who came to Jesus who were not so honest. In John chapter 6 there were some Pharisees who were questioning Jesus about the work of God. In their pride, they asked Him, "What shall we do, so that we may work the works of God?" They were thinking, just like many people today, that what they did determined whether or not the work of God was accomplished. On the surface, this does not look all that bad, but in truth, it is wicked. People think in their natural minds that there is something they have to offer God. God needs nothing we have; He is complete in Himself.

Well, what about the work of God? I've had well meaning Christians say to me, according to James, real faith produces the work of God. Let me say, I could not agree more. Real faith in Christ always produces the work of God. You remember earlier in this chapter that I said; there are many people who want you to do something even if it is wrong. This is exactly the way many Christians feel about the work of God. They want you to get busy. People equate a busy Christian with a faithful Christian. This is not necessarily true. Busyness does not equal faithfulness. Sometimes busyness is a substitute for belief in Christ. The Bible says that anything that is not of faith is sin. Well, if people are busy in their own power and not believing Jesus, it is sin.

In John 6:29, Jesus answered and said to them, "This is the work of God, that you believe in Him whom He has sent." Eternal life is believing in Jesus; the work of God is believing in Jesus. Do you want to do the work of God; believe in Him. Why do people think that they are saved by grace through faith, and then they are to live according to their best efforts after they are saved? You can't please God with your own efforts after you are saved, any more than you could to be saved. It is trusting Him, to live his life in you before you are saved, and after you've are saved, that pleases Him. Only trust Him, I think there is a song by that name isn't there.

I'm going to talk about something that may surprise you. When you believe God for his work, there will be those around you that will become angry with you.

The Bible says that Jesus did not come to judge but to save. When Christians are walking according to the flesh and are trying to work in their own power; many times, they begin to do what Jesus Himself did not do. They begin to judge others based on what they perceive is the work of God. Remember, the work of God is that you believe in Him whom He has sent. You will believe in Him, for whatever He says. He will make His will known to you.

When my wife and I were expecting our first child, we began our first year of seminary. We started with only $540 to our name. We paid our first and last month's rent on our new apartment, turned on our utilities, and paid our deposits. After all this was done, we only had two dollars left. My pastor had shared with me before I left for seminary that I should weigh the cost of a working wife. He meant I should consider whether or not I wanted someone else raising my children. Most of the seminary wives worked outside the home. I am not going to judge what they were doing; I am only going to say what the Lord was telling me. He had convinced us in our heart that Jonni was to remain home.

Jonni and I were at total peace in trusting God by faith to provide for our needs. Our first Sunday at our new church, the great Bellevue Baptist Church in Memphis, Tennessee, a love offering was taken for a need in the church. This was done every year at Bellevue Baptist Church. One Sunday a year was set apart as a day for a special offering and faith promise, and on that day, they trusted God for a large sum of money for special purpose. They asked people not to give what they thought they could afford, but to give what God told them to give. This was called a faith offering. We did what they suggested, we asked, "Lord what do you want us to give?" He told Jonni and me that we were to give $50. If you recall, we only had two dollars. We determined that if the Lord gave us $50, we would give it.

The next day, Monday, a check for $50 came in the mail. This was the first of many miracles concerning money in our lives. We had prayed and asked God how much to give; and then He gave us the money that we were to give. That night, for the first time, I was afraid. I began to doubt God. I said, "Lord you know all we have is two dollars." I told the Lord that I would half the money with Him. $50 divided by two dollars equals $25. That was the way I was thinking. As I lay there, I said, "Lord, anything that causes me this much trouble, I am going to get rid of it." The following day, I took the money to the church and gave it to them. I did not wait for Sunday. That afternoon when I got home, I discovered a check for $100 had come to us. It had been mailed before we received the check for $50. The note that came with the check said, "God told me to give this to you, if you don't need it, give it away." We did not give that check away. I had been thinking division and two dollars into $50 equals $25. God was thinking multiplication, two dollars times $50 equals $100. I like God's way best.

The whole time we were in seminary, I worked, did concerts, preached, but mostly trusted God for his provision. We had three children while we were there, all without maternity insurance, lived in a house, and paid bills. You might say we lived just like everyone else. During this time, as we were going, I had the privilege of seeing God miraculously provide for our family and my wife Jonni never worked outside the home. God told us that we were to give away 20% of every dollar that came into our home. My God is faithful. Because He is faithful, I will believe Him. We still live this way today, trusting Him.

Some of my fellow students, who were truly men of God, almost resented the fact that my wife stayed home with our children. It was almost as if they felt we were not doing our part. Rather than rejoicing in God's provision and believing Him also, they thought that they had to do their part. I am not faulting them for what they did but just giving a warning to those who would judge others.

While I was in seminary, I was asked to head up the Practical Missions program under the president of the seminary. This was a great time in my life. I was able to train young men in how to share their faith and how to trust God in everyday living. We saw many people come into a personal relationship with our Lord Jesus Christ as we were going. I was getting to do what I wanted to do. God was giving me the desire of my heart. I was doing the work of God, believing in Him.

I have shared with you how that believing in Him leads to knowing and having eternal life, His life and how believing in Him leads to His work. I now want to share with you how believing in Him leads to seeing His glory. In John chapter 11 after Mary and Martha contacted Jesus and told Him Lazarus, the one He loved, was about to die, you know the story, Jesus waited three more days, to make sure Lazarus was dead. When Jesus arrived, Mary and Martha told Jesus that if he had only been there, Lazarus would not have died. Jesus told them to remove the stone from the tomb where Lazarus was buried. Martha, the sister of Lazarus, said, "Lord by this time there will be a stench for he has been dead four days." She did not believe that Jesus could raise Lazarus from the dead. In John 11:40, Jesus said to her, "Did I not say to you that if you believe you will see the glory of God?"

Do you see what Jesus is saying here? Today people say they want to see the glory of God. They want to be where the glory is, where the glory comes down. They don't understand that wherever you are if you believe in Him, you will see the glory of God. Believing in Him leads to eternal life, and His work, and seeing the glory of God. This is amazing but true. Lack of faith, not believing in Him, could be the reason we see so little of the glory of God.

The requirement for being saved is righteousness. You must be righteous, as righteous as Jesus is righteous. You may say, "this is impossible". You would be correct. It is impossible to be righteous according to the flesh. If you ask someone who has been born again if they are righteous, I am afraid that some would not know their present position and some who know that they are righteous would not understand how they came to be this way. The Bible tells us how we receive the gift of righteousness. In Romans 10:10, the Bible says, "For with the heart a person believes, resulting in righteousness." Your righteousness comes from God. You believe what He has done. 2 Cor. 5:21 says, *"He who knew no sin became sin so that we might become the righteousness of God in Him."* Righteousness is a gift given, it can only be received, it can't be earned. You cannot even believe God with your old heart; you must have a new heart. He gives you a new heart, not just any heart, His heart. You see and believe what He did and gave to you, His righteousness; you believe that it is yours. It is because of His grace that you have the gift of righteousness. It had nothing to do with you but it was the plan of God from before the foundation of the world to give the gift of righteousness.

I was speaking a while back for a Fellowship of Christian Athletes weekend retreat for coaches and their wives. Also, at this function were several board members for the local FCA. One of the ladies after hearing this message sent me an e-mail with this response. "I have spent years knowing that I am saved, knowing that I am chosen, but always struggling to be even a tiny bit worthy. It has been a tiring and discouraging process. You feel like you are going along at a pretty good clip and then you are saying, thinking or feeling things that are definitely not Christ-like. It's back to feeling like an impostor again and hoping God didn't notice, yeah right. You feel like you need to be washed clean again, every day. Anyway, I am so relieved that my job is to believe! I can do that. I know now, that I am where I am supposed to be in Christ Jesus. Wow!"

This response is not uncommon at all when people begin to understand who they are in Christ and all Christ wants from them is to believe in Him for everything. He is not just my source; He is my life.

When people understand this truth, they will be set free. They will live a life of peace, because they are one with Christ. Are you living and experiencing this life of peace in Christ? Believe in Him, for everything, including what you think He wants you to do. Again, trust Him, for the small things and the large things.

Chapter 7

How To Know The Will of God

For many years I taught and believed that the will of God was something I was to find for myself or even search out. I thought it was all about me. It was as if there was some mystical thing out there and if I was obedient or diligent enough, I could find it. If this is what you think it means to know God's will, you will always feel defeated and go through life thinking you are missing out. Having said that, I unfortunately believe that most Christians find themselves in this group, thinking they have missed God's will.

As I have traveled through the United States and in many countries around the world for the last five decades, I've seen many unfulfilled Christians. Many think they have missed God's perfect will and are living in His permissive will. They think that what they do might stop God from doing what He wants to do. This is a very small view of God.

Let's examine just who God is. First of all, He is eternal. He has no beginning and He has no end. He always has been, and He always will be. He is not bound by time. We are bound by time, but God is not. God created the universe. He did this creation in only six days, and He rested on the seventh day. God exists in three persons: God the Father, God the Son, and God the Holy Spirit. After God created the universe and the earth, and all that is on it, He created man.

When man was disobedient and ate of the tree of the knowledge of good and evil, sin entered the world. As a result of mankind's sin, there was a separation between man and God from man's perspective. Man chose to disobey God, or to say it another way, to not believe Him. Because of this disobedience, or unbelief, fellowship between man and God was broken.

Let's look at what happened. Man believed a lie told by Satan in the form of a serpent to Eve. The deceiver told Eve that the reason YHWH did not want her to eat from the tree of the knowledge of good and evil was because when she did, she WOULD BE LIKE GOD, and know good from evil. This was a partial truth. What is a partial truth; it is a total lie.

There were two problems with what the serpent told Eve. The first was that she had to do something to be like God. This was a total lie. She was created in His image and had His life breathed into her in Geneses

2:7. Man was not created as the animals were. They were created and told to be fruitful and multiply and God said it was good. They were created alive. Man was created in God's image and had the very life-giving Spirit of God breathed into him. Do you see the difference, the animals were given life. Man, however, was given LIFE, the very life of YHWH Himself.

There was nothing Eve or Adam needed to do or could do to be like God, they were like Him from eternity past when He chose them and it was brought to fruition when He created them in His image. Eve believed the same lie that people believe today, you have to do something to be somebody.

The second problem with the lie that Satan told Eve was maybe even more sinister. He said you will know right from wrong. This was in fact true. After Eve and Adam ate from the Tree of the Knowledge of Good and Evil, they did, in fact, know right from wrong. They did know good from evil. You may say what is wrong with that; in fact, that is what is taught in churches by well-meaning people all over the world.

So, what is the problem? God never intended anyone to go through life discerning right from wrong to control their actions. He wanted people to walk in His life given to them as their life and to be controlled by His Spirit which was given to them as a Helper, Comforter, and One who imparts wisdom.

As a result of eating from the Tree of the Knowledge of Good and Evil there was indeed separation of man from God and fellowship with man and God was broken. It was Adam and Eve hiding from God. Man separated himself from God, God did not separate Himself from Man.

In the cool of the day YHWH and Adam and Eve would walk as one in the Garden. On this fateful day YHWH was in the garden but Adam and Eve did not show up, they were hiding from God. Do you see the humor here? How could anyone hide from the all-knowing God?

YHWH said, "Adam, Eve, where are you?" They answered and said, "We are hiding." How silly, but that was what they were thinking. There was separation and broken fellowship but it was all from man's side. Man hid from God but God sought man. Not only was there separation with YHWH but there was loss of fellowship. Mankind was dead to the fact that his life was in God. Man hid from YHWH and did not desire fellowship with the one who created them and loved them. YHWH not only desired fellowship to be restored, He was the one who was going to restore it.

Before Adam and Eve had willfully disobeyed God, they were naked and not ashamed. Now they were naked and ashamed and tried through their own efforts to deal with their nakedness. They covered themselves with leaves. Man was trying to deal with his sin through his own efforts. This goes on today through religion and trying to obey the LAW thinking that would make you right with God. It did not work then and it does not work now.

Because of the unconditional love of God the Father, Christ the Son and God the Holy Spirit toward Adam and Eve and all of man, something happened that had not happened before. Blood was shed. Up until this point nothing had ever died in the Garden. But now an innocent animal was killed and its skin was taken to make a covering for Adam and Eve's nakedness. This was God restoring fellowship and relationship with Man.

The act by YHWH of the shedding of innocent blood was the first picture of the cross in scripture. It was a picture of what had already occurred in eternity but was yet to happen in time. It was a picture of Romans 5:18,19.

18 So then as through one transgression there resulted condemnation to all men, even so through one act of righteousness there resulted justification of life to all men.

19 For as through the one man's disobedience the many were made sinners, even so through the obedience of the One the many will be made righteous.

This was done and finished before time existed but it was finished in time for all men on the cross when Christ uttered, "It is finished." It was revealed in 2ⁿᵈ Corinthians 5:21 when it says, "He who knew no sin became sin so that we might become the righteousness of God in Him.

I no longer tell people what we are to do to be right with God. I now tell people what the Godhead, the Trinity has done on our behalf to bring us into this right relationship with Them. The three in one chose us before the foundation of the world and in love, have predestined us to be adopted as sons. I now ask people to believe what He has done for them and receive the gift of His life that has been given to them. Believe and faith in the Greek is the same word. Believe is the verb in English and faith is the noun. It was the faith of Christ that justifies and gives life as I have already mentioned in an earlier chapter.

The Bible says, "For by grace you have been saved through faith, it is a gift of God not as a result of works that any man should boast". Grace and faith are both gifts of God. God gives grace because He wants to. He also gives you the gift of faith. You can't even believe in your own power. The Word says that faith is also a gift of God. You don't boast in what you have not done, you praise Him for what He has done.

Jesus said in John 6:44, "no one can come to me unless the Father who sent me draws him". In John 6:65 He says again, "For this reason I have said to you, that no one can come to me unless it has been granted him from the Father". Do you see what He is saying here? Your salvation is totally from Him. It is all Him; it is none of you. It is totally a gift of God.

Through revelation by the Father through the Holy Spirit, Jesus has been made known to you. He has revealed to you what He has done and given to you and you believe Him that it is true and finished. It is all God and none of man that brings man into this right relationship with Him.

If Christians believe that God has revealed Himself to them and has given them eternal life, (His life), then why wouldn't they believe that He would reveal His will to them?

What Is God's Will?

God's will is in knowing and being, not in doing. In the United States of America, people are proud of what they do. People believe that you should be able to measure what you have accomplished. They feel the same way about God's will. They feel that God's will is found in what you do and not in who you are. This is tragic!

In the world, people are searching for something better. People are searching for a better job, a better house, a better car, and sadly sometimes even a better spouse. They are constantly looking for the open door of opportunity. I've heard it said, "Opportunity only knocks once". They don't want to miss this knock. Hearing the knock of opportunity, according to the world, requires a keen ear. In other words, it is totally up to you. Don't miss it; it may not come around again. It saddens me to say that this is how most people in the church also think. They have made the will of God something that *you* find and not something that God reveals. God is a loving Father. As a loving Father, He reveals to us what is best for us. He does this because he wants to. It brings Him pleasure to bless us.

I am a father and I am also a grandfather. As a father, I made my will known to my children. My children did not get out of bed in the morning and say to themselves; "Today I will seek my father's will." What my children did was, get out of bed and go to the table to eat breakfast. They believed that their earthly father would make provision for them, for that day and for everyday. They relished in their relationship with me. They were my children and I loved them. Their relationship with me was not based on what they could do for me. Their relationship with me was based on the fact that they were my children; nothing else was needed. Because I loved my children, I revealed my will to them. My will was not something they feared or doubted or sought-after, it was in someone they knew. I revealed it to them, because I loved them.

I am certainly not a better father than God the Father. God wants us to know Him, and who we are in Him and the fact that He loves us. As we believe Him, we are given His mind. YHWH said in Hebrews chapter 8 and chapter 10 that He has written His laws on our minds and on our hearts. He also says this in Jeremiah chapter 31. We have the mind of Christ; we have a new heart, and we have a new nature. The new nature that we have is literally the nature of Christ. Our old nature has died with Him on the cross. We were buried with Him, and we were raised with Him to walk in newness of life. Not just any life, but His life. There is another way of saying this, "we think like Him". He has exchanged His life with us. The old man that you were, no longer exist. We don't have a changed life; we have an exchanged life. Our life has been exchanged with the life of Christ. According to Colossians 3:4, Jesus Christ is my life.

How then do we know God's will? That is a very good question. It is a question that everyone has probably asked. We must start by understanding that knowing God's will is not about what we do, but it is about whom we know and who we are. You are a child of

God, you are holy, you are righteous, and you have the mind of Christ. Because you have the mind of Christ you now think like Him.

I want to ask you a question, "What is the desire of your heart?" The Bible says in Psalm 37: 3, 4, " Trust in the Lord and do good; dwell in the land and cultivate faithfulness. Delight yourself in the Lord; and He will give you the desires of your heart." These verses are some of my favorite in the Bible. What does this say? Trust is another word for believe. When you trust someone, you believe what he says. Do you believe what Jesus says about who you are in Him? Do you believe that you have His mind and nature? Do you believe that you have His heart? It says to do good. Jesus said only God is good. What is it that we do that is good? It's very simple, Hebrews 11:6 says, "without faith it is impossible to please Him". The only good thing we can do is to believe Him. In the Greek, as I have stated before, the word believe and the word faith mean the same thing. Believing God pleases Him. Verse three also says that we are to cultivate faithfulness while we are dwelling in the land. God wants us to simply believe Him while we go about our daily lives. As you begin to believe Him for small things you will learn to believe Him for everything. This is cultivating faithfulness. Remember, there is nothing that is a big thing to God.

In verse four the word delight means to be happy about or to make merry over. It literally means to be happy over the Lord. It comes from the root-word soft, or delicate, or dainty. I believe this is the idea where we can get the song *Jesus loves me, this I know for the*

Bible tells me so. Little ones to Him belong; they are
weak but He is strong.

When I think that I am weak, dainty, and delicate and
that He is strong, it makes me very happy. My joy and
my happiness are found in Christ. When I know that I
am loved by Him and that I am made holy in Him and
that I am righteous in Him; it makes me delight in Him.
In whom are you delighting? As you believe in Him,
and delight yourself in Him, He will give you the desire
of your heart. A simple way of putting this is believe
in Him; be happy in Him; and do anything you want to.
This seems almost too good to be true, but it is true.
God Himself will reveal his desires for your life
through your desires. Another way of saying this is
that he will make His desires your desires. I say,
"Believe Him and do whatever you want."

Manipulating God's Will

In the church today, I am afraid people are being manipulated into doing things that they were never called to do. As a result of this, people are tired; they feel like failures; and they want to quit. What would happen if we just said, "If someone loves children and would like to work with them in the nursery and in preschool please come now? And then we said if you really enjoy serving others and would like to cut grass or clean the building; would you please come forward? Those of you who have a great desire and are gifted to teach, would you please come over here? Now those of you who are gifted in the area of evangelism and this is the desire of your heart would you please come and go with me."

I can hear you now, "Pastor, have you lost your mind?" Well, I will answer you. "No, I have not lost my mind." I believe that when people are given the opportunity to do what it is that they really want to do, they will do it with joy in their heart. They will not quit, they will not burn out and they will not drop out. It will not be someone else's ministry for them; it will be their own desire. What a joy it is when your ministry is what you really desire. Some people would think that this is just living in a dream world. As a pastor, I know the other way is not working very well. The day of a committee coming together and asking, who can **we get** to do this, must become a thing of the past.

The reason that you don't see this happening in the church and other places is because people don't really believe that God can get things done without our help.

They don't believe that God is sovereign. People may believe that God is sovereign over salvation, but think from that point on it is all about what we do. God is telling us in His Word, that we can trust Him to reveal His will to us and we will like it. His will for us is what we would choose if we knew enough to do so. We must learn to hear Him when He speaks, and to recognize that still small voice that spoke to the prophets of old. God still speaks in a still small voice, and it is one that you will recognize as you are delighting in Him and believing in Him. You can trust Him.

There is one other thing that I want to share concerning knowing the will of God. It is, relax. Did you say relax? Yes, that is exactly what I said. Relax, chill out; don't fret the small stuff. You see; it is all small stuff to God. If He did create the universe, and give you His life and make you holy and righteous, what is there that He can't do? Let your desire be to know Him. Know who you are in Him and know that He loves you. Also know that there is nothing you need to do to please Him because He is already pleased with you. It was and is your faith in Him that pleases Him. As these things begin to become reality in your walk, you are going to be blown away by all that you find you get to do. Sometimes you may even be surprised at what you want to do. What you want to do may change as you come to know your identity in Him.

One last thing, do not worry about missing God's will for your life. You could not miss it even if you tried. If you could, that would make you bigger than God and you are most certainly not bigger than God. Not only is He bigger than you; He cares about you so much that He will do what ever is necessary to bring you to the end of yourself. Don't try and second-guess when things don't seem to work out. Sometimes, for things to have their full beauty, they must be outlined in black. God is the master painter of your life. Trust Him! God is in control and He will not let you miss His will. He is directing you as you walk in Him.

You may say, "But what if I wasn't walking in Him?" Don't worry about it. He is and will always be in control. I say again, trust Him and do what you want. He has given you His mind. As you become totally dependent on Him, His will for your life will truly become the desire of your heart. Your desires will be fulfilled because He is the one living His life in you. Believe Him for your desires, for your happiness, for your fulfillment, for your very life. Know that His life

is your life, His position is your position, and His

sonship is your sonship.

Chapter 8

Delay
Why Jesus Tarries

The very name of this chapter brings feelings of fear and trembling. Let's get some things straight. I don't like waiting. I especially don't like waiting when I am hurting. When I am hurting, nothing seems fast enough. I don't like waiting in the doctor's office, I don't like waiting in the pharmacy, and I don't like waiting for the medicine to work. I want to feel better now. That is just the way I am, and I imagine that you are the same way.

When I have the pleasure of going to a really fine restaurant, I am not just going to get food. There is expectation of something great that is about to happen. I may have heard that they have a great chef who is gifted at taking the ordinary and making it extra ordinary. He knows what others do not and the meal is truly worth the wait. While I am waiting, I dwell on the ecstasy of what is coming. I talk about it and look forward to it with excitement. I know that what is about to come is worth the wait. This is what we should believe about God. He knows; He is preparing something beautiful and wonderful for us, and it will be worth the wait.

When I go to a fast food restaurant, I don't have high expectations of quality, but I do have expectations of hot food now. Taste is almost a non-issue. When I don't get my food in what I think is a timely fashion, I get upset. Isn't this silly. We want what we want because we want it and pout when we don't get it, *now*.

In other words, we act just like children. I am sorry to say that many Christians are no different. We pray in just the same way that we order fast food. We want what we want *now* and we don't really have any great expectations of God doing great and mighty things that are a marvel to behold.

In the day of digital cameras, we have forgotten about the role of film developers. In the past, people used to take their film to the best developers that were available to them when they cared about the outcome of the pictures. They would either mail their pictures to a fine developer, or they would drop them off with someone they knew to be expert in this field. They would then wait because they knew they were about to receive something special.

Faith and film are very much alike. They both develop

best in the dark. The results of both are out of your

control. My flesh doesn't like this. I don't like waiting,

and I don't like being in the dark. Sometimes, however,

we trust our film developer, more than we do the God

who loves us. This is both tragic and very sad.

In John 11 verses 1-5 we see the story of Lazarus.

*John 11:1 Now a certain man was sick, Lazarus of
Bethany, the village of Mary and her sister Martha.
2 It was the Mary who anointed the Lord with
ointment, and wiped His feet with her hair, whose
brother Lazarus was sick.
3 So the sisters sent word to Him, saying, "Lord, behold,
he whom You love is sick."
4 But when Jesus heard this, He said, "This sickness is
not to end in death, but for the glory of God, so that the
Son of God may be glorified by it."
5 Now Jesus loved Martha and her sister and Lazarus.*
We see that Lazarus was about to die. Mary and

Martha sent for Jesus. They believed Jesus could heal

him, but they believed He had to be in their presence

to do it. In other words, they had to see it with their own eyes. They had faith, but it was faith that needed to be developed. Jesus knew that their faith must be developed in the dark totally out of their control. I can relate to this, can you? I sometimes believe that not only must Jesus answer my prayer, but He also must answer my prayer the way I tell Him.

The disciples had their own problems with faith. They thought, based on past experiences, if Jesus went back to Judea, He would surely be stoned. They thought He would die. They did not understand that was exactly what He had been called to do. Even though He had been with them for nearly three years and He had told them many times that He must die; they still did not believe and understand. They were trying to control circumstances that were out of their control. Let me ask you a question. Are you trying to control circumstances that you were never intended to control? God does not want you to control any of your circumstances; He wants you to trust Him. He will put you in situations that are out of your control so that you will learn to trust Him

Facts of Delay

There is something about Jesus that I don't always understand. It is that He often delays. In John 11:6-7, Mary and Martha sent word to Jesus, that the one He loved, Lazarus, was about to die. They wanted Him to come quickly. Jesus waited two days and then said, "Let's go." He waited until He knew that Lazarus was dead and buried. Lazarus was dead. To Mary and Martha, all must have seemed hopeless. Are there things in your life that appear hopeless to you? If there are, then this is for you. Jesus not only *allows* us to come to the end of our hope in the flesh; He even *causes* us to come to the end of our hope in the flesh.

I am not going to go back and cover old ground; I am just going to assume that you know Jesus is God in the flesh. Many times, we expect God to operate on our timetable and according to our plan. We think we know best. When we pray, we already think we know how things should turn out. We want God to be just like the person that takes our order at McDonald's. We want what we want when we want it and we will pout if it does not turn out like we want it. We know what we want Him to do for us and we want it now. We know how we want it done, our way. We know why we want Him to do what we want, because we want it. We know where we want it done. We want it done wherever we tell Him.

I myself am still guilty of this at times. I know that He knows what I need and that He loves me, but sometimes I still tell Him what to do. When this happens, He treats me just like He did Mary and Martha and the disciples; He loves me and is patient with me. Boy, am I glad that He is God and that I am not.

When the people of Israel asked Yahweh to set them free from Pharaoh and Egypt, He delayed. In delaying, God proved five things to all people. He proved *He loved His people*, and *He would have His way.* He also proved that *He had power over the elements*, natural and supernatural, and over governments. He proved

He was a God that would forgive. Many Egyptians repented and came out of Egypt with the Israelites. He treated them like His own because they were. One last thing God proved by delaying; He *proved that he would provide* for His people. By waiting, the children of Israel left with untold riches. God gave His people favor with the Egyptians and they lavished gifts on them before they departed. Had they left when they wanted to leave, they would have left penniless and powerless.

Frustrations of Delay

Unbelievable as this may sound, Mary and Martha rebuked Jesus for not coming sooner. In verse 21, Martha said, *"Lord if you had been here, my brother would not have died."* In verse 32, Mary fell at Jesus feet and said the same thing Martha said. They both had a measure of faith in Christ, but very weak faith. In their minds, there was no hope. Jesus loved them so much that He allowed them to become totally broken. He didn't get mad at them.

Even the multitudes, that did not know Jesus, had an opinion about the situation. This is no different than people today judging Christ based on what they think He should do. In verse 37 some of the people said, *"Could not this man, who opened the eyes of the blind man, have kept this man also from dying?"* Mary, Martha, and the multitudes did not know the true nature of Christ, but they soon would. They did not know that He was Lord even over death.

Do you know the true nature of Christ? I'm going to tell you something. As a believer, you have the true nature of Christ; He has given you His nature. You are like Him and you think like Him; you have His mind. Listen to the Spirit as He convicts you of your righteousness in Him.

Many times, we are upset, and we want to rebuke Jesus for not doing things our way. Sometimes we even become disappointed with Jesus. In the end, when we see what Jesus has done, we are glad that He did not do things our way.   What I'm going to tell you next may seem strange to you. Go ahead; tell Him your frustrations, He can handle it. He won't stop loving you.

Fruits of Delay

I am just going to say it. Delay develops our faith. It helps us to see the big picture and to learn to trust God. In John 11:8-9, in the face of darkness and much disbelief the disciples said they would go with Jesus. They believed that Jesus would die, and that they also would die. They were loyal to Jesus, but they did not truly believe Him. This is the way many people are today. They are loyal to Jesus, but they're not truly willing to trust Him with their lives. They don't truly believe that His life is their life. They don't believe that Jesus loves them and knows what is best for them. They think that what happens with Jesus is based on what they do.

Jesus told his disciples in John 11:15, that for their sakes, He was glad that He was not there so that they might believe. When the disciples arrived at the tomb where Lazarus had been laid, they knew three things. They knew Lazarus was really dead and there was much grieving going on. They also knew that Jesus had much compassion. The Bible says in John 11: 35 that *Jesus wept*. Many believers are grieving today. Know this, Jesus cares and will weep with you. He also is in control and will bless you with Himself. It is okay to grieve, but when you see the glory of God, the grieving will stop. Ask Jesus to show you His glory.

The disciples, along with Mary and Martha, did not really believe that Jesus could bring Lazarus back from the dead. Jesus told Martha that Lazarus would rise from the dead. Martha replied to Jesus that she knew that Lazarus would rise on the *Day of Resurrection*. In John 11:25- 26, Jesus said to her, *"I am the resurrection and the life; he who believes in Me will live even if he dies, and everyone who lives and believes in Me will never die. Do you believe this?"* Martha, just like so many today, believed in Jesus but didn't really believe Jesus. When Jesus *spoke* these words of resurrection and new life to those who believed in Him, Martha's perspective changed. She called her sister Mary and said, "Jesus wants to see you."

When Mary came to the place where Jesus was, she fell at his feet and said, *"Lord if you had only been here, my brother would not have died."* She believed that Jesus could heal but not that He could give life. She believed Jesus, but only to a point. That's the problem I see in the church today. People believe that Jesus will give salvation, but they don't understand that He gives

us His life.

When did this take place? It took place in time at the

cross, but it really took place from eternity past before

anything was created. Romans 5:17-19 speaks of what

the last Adam, Christ did for all men.

> *17 For if by the transgression of the one, death*
> *reigned through the one, much more those who*
> *receive the abundance of grace and of the gift of*
> *righteousness will reign in life through the One,*
> *Jesus Christ.*
> *18 So then as through one transgression there*
> *resulted condemnation to all men, even so*
> *through one act of righteousness there resulted*
> *justification of life to all men.*
> *19 For as through the one man's disobedience*
> *the many were made sinners, even so through the*
> *obedience of the One the many will be made*
> *righteous.*

Do all men know this; no. Have all men believed this;

no. Have all men received the gift of His life that has

been given to all men and walk in it; no. Do they need

to believe that Christ has given His life for them and to them to benefit from what He has done; yes. Is it finished whether they believe it or not; yes it is. It was finished from the cross. I now tell men what Christ has done, what He has given to all men and encourage them to believe it for themselves. I don't tell them what Christ will do for them if they do something for Him, BELIEVE.

I also tell them what Christ did from the cross, FORGIVE. It is done, completed, can't be done again. We need to believe this wonderful truth that God has forgiven all men because they know not what they do. Christians will benefit from knowing this truth and believing that it applies to them also.

Neither Mary nor Martha could make themselves believe in Jesus in their own power. The Holy Spirit of God is the One who reveals to us that Jesus gives us His life. Jesus was about to demonstrate through the power of the Holy Spirit that Lazarus would live again.

40 Jesus said to her, "Did I not say to you that if you believe, you will see the glory of God?" 41 So they removed the stone. Then Jesus raised His eyes, and said, "Father, I thank You that You have heard Me. 42 "I knew that You always hear Me; but because of the people standing around I said it, so that they may believe that You sent Me."
43 When He had said these things, He cried out with a loud voice, "Lazarus, come forth."

In John 11:4 Jesus said, *"This sickness is not to end in death, but for the glory of God, so that the Son of God may be glorified by it."* Are there things that are going on in your life that seem terrible? Know this; everything that He does in your life is for His glory. Believe Him, even when you don't understand.

Jesus also said in John 11:40, *"That if you believe, you will see the glory of God."*   There's no doubt about the glory of God; the only doubt is if you will believe Him. We've seen in earlier chapters that when you believe, you will know eternal life. John 17:3, eternal life is knowing the Father and the Son whom He has sent.

We've also seen that when you believe, you will do the work of God, John 6:29. We are now seeing that when you believe, you see the glory of God. It's all by faith; it is a gift of God, not as a result of works that anyone should boast. This whole incident started for the Glory of God and will end up with the Glory of God.

When Jesus raised his eyes and prayed to the Father, He thanked Him that He heard Him. Jesus said in verse 42, *"I knew that You always hear Me; but because of the people standing around I said it, so that they may believe that You sent Me."* He prayed according to the power of the Father. It was what the Father was going to do through Him. The same thing is true today in our lives. Jesus believed the Father, and the glory of God was seen. We are to believe the Father just like Jesus did, and we, also, will see the glory of God.

When Jesus cried out in a loud voice, "Lazarus come forth"; everyone around saw the glory of God. I believe lives were changed on that day. Mary and Martha's lives were most certainly changed. They had seen life come out of death. When Jesus caused you to be raised from the dead with Him and you experienced the glory of God, your life changed. Mary and Martha were never the same. When you have been given the life of Christ, your life will never be the same.

In verses 44 and 45 we see some of the most dramatic things that ever happened in the Bible.

44 The man who had died came forth, bound hand and foot with wrappings, and his face was wrapped around with a cloth. Jesus said to them, "Unbind him, and let him go." 45 Therefore many of the Jews who came to Mary, and saw what He had done, believed in Him.

Jesus told them to unbind him and let him go. He came forth bound hand and foot with wrappings. Lazarus no longer needed the grave clothes. He was no longer dead; he was alive. When people trust Christ today, they no longer need the bindings of the law. Romans 8:2 says, *"For the law of the spirit of life in Christ Jesus has set me free from the law of sin and death."*

I'm so glad this is in the Bible. You see what this is saying; you have been set free from the law of sin and death. People that are alive in Christ don't need the law any more. Those that had seen the glory of God understood this. They knew it would be silly for Lazarus to hop through life. He had been made alive; he was no longer dead. Maybe people, that think you still need the law to rule your life after you have trusted Christ, have never truly seen the glory of God, or possibly they have seen God's glory but just didn't believe it. The Bible says it is for freedom that you have been set free. If the law binds you, you are not free. You don't need law telling you what to do any more; you have the very mind of Christ. You think like Him; His life is your life.

The last fruit of delay that we're going to look at is *growth in absolute dependence on Jesus.* I have heard people say, "Jesus does His part, and we must do our part". They use the story of Lazarus being raised from the dead as their example. They say, "Jesus brought Lazarus back to life but people there rolled the stone away." They thought that Jesus needed help. This could not be further from the truth; Jesus didn't need the peoples help! He does not need our help today.

There is nothing that anyone can add to the grace of God. He does not need our help in any way. It is no longer what we have to do; it is what we get to do. We will do things, and we will like it, but it is because we believe Him and have seen His glory that we desire to minister and serve with Him. It is truly now the desire of our heart.

In concluding this chapter, I want to discuss a problem that I see. People think that they are not strong enough to face problems or to serve God. That is not the problem at all. The problem is not that they are not strong enough; it is that they are not weak enough. People thrash about struggling while they are trying to do things for God or to solve problems themselves. When we come to the end of ourselves, Jesus will work. We try everything, and when we are physically and emotionally spent, we say there's nothing else to do but to pray and trust God. We end up where we should have started.

The reason that God tarries in regard to your life is because He is bringing you to a place of absolute dependence on Him. He wants you to see and also experience His glory. Have you become weak enough for God to work in your life? Are you willing to surrender your life totally to Him? If you are, you will see the glory of God in your life, around your life, and on your life. You must believe Him in all situations. As a result of your believing Him and personally experiencing the glory of God, many will see the results of what Jesus has done and believe Him.

Chapter 9

Being A Witness

Can you remember when you first gave your heart to Jesus? I can, it seems like it was just a little while ago. It was, however, many, many years ago. I still remember coming back from a meeting of young Christian college students and realizing that there was something terribly missing in my life. I was lying on my bed, and seemingly out of no place, I shouted out the words, "Save me, Jesus". A wonderful thing immediately happened; He did save me. I did not realize at that point that we were saved by His life, but I knew I wanted Him. I later came to know what had been given me from eternity past, His life as my life.

I did not understand all that had just taken place in my life, but I was aware that something mighty had just happened. I was instantly overcome with emotion, and it seemed as if burdens had been lifted off of me. I felt free. I did not know it then but I "was" free. There was an urge to tell someone what had just happened in my life. It was very early in the morning and I proceeded to share what had just happened to me with a childhood friend. I called him right then. He understood perfectly because he had been a Christian for a long time; he even went on to explain what was happening in my life.

I want to tell you some things that he did not say to me. He did not say, "Craig, now tell everyone that you meet or can think of what has happened to you". As a matter of fact, he did not tell me to do anything. He just rejoiced with me. He seemed to be as thrilled as I was. The next day, I began a life long road of telling people about the love of Jesus and what it was that He did for me.

I did not know what you called telling people about Jesus. I thought it was just something that people did when they received and believed in Jesus. I shared my relationship with Christ with all my friends and family, and with most people that I came in contact with. It was who I was and not what I did.

I later found out that people called it "witnessing," and I also discovered that it was something that all Christians were "expected to do." Witnessing became part of my job description as a Christian instead of the desire of my heart as a believer in Christ. It became something that had to be worked at instead of lived out. It also lost its appeal and I lost my zeal for telling people about Jesus.

Today, the word witness is one of the most misunderstood words in the Bible. Most people think that witnessing is what you do rather than who you are. In order to clear up this misunderstanding, we need to examine again who we are in Christ. The Bible says that in Christ we are holy. Colossians 3:12 says, "*So, you have been chosen of God, holy*". The Word holy means to set apart. When God chose you, He set you apart. When did He do this, before the foundation of the world, Ephesians 1:4. The Word that is used is the same word that means saint. You have been made a saint of God. This is also the word that is used for sanctified. You are sanctified, and holy, and set apart based on what He did and not on what you did. It was, and is, all Him.

The Bible also says that you were made righteous in Him based on His actions, not your actions. Your righteousness is by grace through faith in Him. Romans 10:10 says, *"with the heart a person believes, resulting in righteousness, and with the mouth he confesses, resulting in salvation."* Your righteousness is every bit as much by grace through faith in Him as is your salvation. It is not just how God sees you; it is how you truly are.

Not only are you holy and righteous, but you also have a new mind and a new heart. You think like Him. The Bible says in Hebrews 10:18 that He has written His laws on your mind and heart. You now think differently; you think like Him. You think differently because you are different. You are different because you have a new nature. In Romans six, we see that the old you died with Christ, and you have been buried with Christ and raised to walk in newness of life with Him. Romans 5-8 says that we have a new nature. We don't have a changed nature, or an improved nature; we have a different nature. Our old dead nature died with Christ and was buried with Him. When we were raised to walk in newness of life, we began walking in our new nature. Our new nature is literally the nature of Christ. So now we see who we are. We are holy and we are righteous and we have the heart and mind of Christ. We also have His nature. We think just like Him because we have His mind. This does not mean that we don't still deal with the flesh. We do, but that is for another discussion. What we do does not always reflect who we are.

In Acts 1:8, Jesus said, "...*But you shall receive power when the Holy Spirit has come upon you; and you shall be my witnesses in Judea and Samaria and even the remotest part of the earth.*" When we examine what this verse says, we see several things that are a statement of fact. The first thing we see is that we shall receive power when the Holy Spirit has come upon us. The power we receive is the same power from which Jesus operated. He did nothing in His own power; everything He did was through the power of the Holy Spirit. He did only what the Father told Him. Do you see what a big deal this is? The very power that created the universe is living in you. The same Holy Spirit who empowered Jesus empowers you. You may be thinking this could not be so. If it is not so, then the Bible is not true, but the Bible is true, and you have received the power of the Holy Spirit. It is a fact.

The following statement is one of the biggest things ever said to Christians. Jesus also said in Acts 1:8, *"You shall be my witnesses."* Notice that this is not a command. Also notice that *witness* is a noun and not a verb. This is not a command telling you to do something, but it is a statement of fact concerning your being. Jesus is telling His disciples who they will become and not what they are to do.

When I first trusted Christ, my desire was to tell people about Jesus. I did not know very much but I knew that Jesus loved me, and I wanted everyone to know Him. I read my Bible because I wanted to and I talked about

Jesus because it was the desire of my heart. It was who I was. I had never been to a witnessing class, nor had anyone told me at that time, what I should do. I was a totally new creation in Christ; I had become a witness in Christ.

Today, most Christians have been taught that witnessing is what they do. This is exactly the opposite of what the Bible says. The Bible says we are witnesses and because of this fact, we do witness. The word witness means martyr. The Greek word for martyr is martyr. There is only one thing that a martyr does; he dies. We don't go to seminars where we are taught to go out and die. If people understood that the requirement for being a witness was to die, there would not be many volunteers. Here is the good news. You don't have to die again; you have already died with

Christ. Not only have you died, but also, you have been raised to walk in newness of life with Him.

As a pastor for many years, I have realized that the most effective time for evangelism in a person's life is right after he comes to know Christ. His life is different, he knows it, and so does everyone else. People see the difference in his life, and he wants to talk about the One who has made him different. He wants to talk about Jesus. He is not religious; his life has been exchanged with the life of Christ.

Many friends and relatives of a new believer also come to know Christ because of the testimony of an exchanged life. In fact, statistics tell us that over 92% of people who trust Christ do it because of the direct or indirect witness of a friend or relative. That should speak volumes to us about what real evangelism is.

Then what happens? If people are effective witnesses after they are first saved, why do they lose their zeal for telling people about their new life in Christ? I believe I know why this happens. Religion and law tell people that they must do something in order to be someone. Grace tells people who they are in Christ. Their life takes on the characteristics of the One who lives inside them. Another way of saying this is that Grace leads to effective witnessing and that law leads away from effective witnessing. When someone shares Christ because he thinks he should, it becomes pressed, dry and stale. In other words, it is hard. When you share the new life that you now have in Christ, it is normal and easy. It does not seem any more like working than going fishing does. It is what you get to do, it is who you are. When someone talks about the One who loves him and tells people that He loves them also, others want to know Him. It is both real and effective. For the rest of this chapter I'm going to share some experiences with witnessing as a way of life. I'm going to take the personal privilege of sharing things I have seen in my own life.

One of the first people who came to know Jesus, as a direct result of a personal witness from me was a young man named Steve. He was someone that I had known for a while, but I did not know him well. I was at a University of Georgia football game, and the girl I was with asked me to begin to pray for this man named Steve. I said okay and did not think too much about it. It was soon after that I started a new job as a counselor with the new Youth Development Center in Athens. When I showed up for orientation, I found out that this man named Steve was also going to be working there. We were sent on an errand to pick up some tables and chairs for our grand opening. As we were driving in his station wagon, he said, "Tell me about this Jesus thing". It was while we were driving and it was totally unforced. That friend's life was transformed and he has walked in who he is in Christ for over 40 years now.

In the first chapter of this book, I talked about sharing my relationship with Christ on the back of an army truck going into the field while I was in the Army Reserves. A young man named Chris was listening to me while I was talking to someone else and went home and gave his life to Christ. Not only was it not work talking to Chris, I was not even talking to Chris. God will use His Word wherever and however He will. Chris was a pastor for many years in a large church in Atlanta. God is certainly good. I had the joy of talking with Chris some time back and was encouraged at how God is continuing to use his life.

When I was in seminary, I began teaching an 11th grade Sunday school class at Bellevue Baptist Church. Bellevue was a great church and had a great pastor who became my friend. His name was Dr. Adrian Rogers. He has gone home to be with the Lord now, but he influenced my life greatly over all these years. He corresponded with me off and on until his ultimate home going, as I am sure he did with many others.

Having said that about Bellevue and Dr. Rogers let me say it was a great privilege to teach at Bellevue. I was going to learn a lesson while teaching there that would stay with me all these years. My new class was made up of eight young men. There were three 11th grade classes to keep them small. On the first day, I shared about the opportunity of influencing friends and family with the good news of the Gospel of Christ.

There was a young man named Ron in our class who did not say much. He was tall and walked stooped over. He had a bad peroxide job on his hair, and it had turned almost orange. His face was broken out, and he even had a hard time looking at you when he spoke to you.

I was going to learn a great deal from Ron, but I did not know it. Ron believed me when I told him that God loved him, and he began telling all his friends that He loved them also. One Sunday, Ron brought a visitor with him to Sunday school. After the class was over, they were waiting for me as I left the classroom. Ron brought him to me and told me that his friend needed Jesus. I had the joy of sharing Christ with his friend and watch him being birthed into the kingdom of God. This kind of thing went on all year with Ron and began to affect others in our class.

As a result of Ron's witness, another young man named John came to me and said, "I really admire Ron, and I am humbled by him". I told John that he should go tell Ron what he had just told me. He did just that. Our class grew to over 30 that year as a result of people living out of their new relationship in Christ. It was not me and not Ron; it was not even our efforts. It was, in fact, Christ living His life in all of us.

It is hard to condense a life into such a short space, so I am only going to share a few more experiences of living as a witness with the power of the Holy Spirit. While I was serving with a church in Arkansas, I would regularly visit all the newcomers to our town. I would go to the city hall and get a list of all the people who had just gotten their utilities turned on. There was one house in particular that I would attempt to visit on a regular basis. Each time I would drive by, I would be overcome with the idea that I should not go there. This was unusual, but I obeyed. Some weeks later I told myself that I was going to that house tonight, no matter what. When I arrived at the house, I went and knocked on the front door. A young married woman named Margie came to the door. I said, "Hello, I am Craig Snyder from the First Baptist Church. I have come to welcome you to our town and to share with you how much God loves you." I remember she had the strangest look on her face.

She let me in and took me into the kitchen. Her husband was bringing in groceries from their car. They had arrived at the back door at the same time that I had arrived at the front door. Margie and I sat at her kitchen table, and I shared the Gospel of Christ with her while her husband proceeded to put away the groceries. He went on to cook his supper while Margie and I continued to talk about a relationship with Christ. He then went into the living room and began to watch TV, but in the mean time, Margie gave her life to

Christ. We baptized her and saw her begin to live her new life in Christ. She was a "different" person. Her husband was not pleased at all with the new Margie. He made it very difficult on her and demanded that she stop going to church.

A good while later, I ran into Margie in a department store. She shared with me how God had been growing her in her new relationship with Him in spite of her situation at home. She also told me why she had been so surprised to see me when I first knocked on her door.

I am not about to knock any group here, I am just going to tell you what Margie told me. She had been a Catholic and had gone to a church and was told that she could not attend there because it was not her parish. She was told she would have to attend another one closer to where she lived. She was not happy about this because it was made up of mostly older folks. She had said to the Lord that day, "Lord, if I am not a Christian, send someone to tell me". That was the very night that I showed up at her door. Remember I said I had not stopped at her house earlier because I had a feeling that I should not go there. God was teaching me just what it meant to let Him live His life in me and for Him to make me His witness.

You may have the idea that God will only use you as a witness when everything is going well. I want to dispel that idea right here. My family and I were headed from Arkansas to the home of my parents in Athens, Georgia, on a hot summer day. We were about 60 miles from our home in Maumelle, close to Little Rock, when the transmission of my car began to go out. We were able to limp back to Maumelle and someone in our church graciously bought us a rebuilt transmission that very day. I was rejoicing for this blessing and for the fact that we would only be one day late going to see my folks.

The next day we set out for Athens again. It was a very hot that afternoon, and all three of our boys had chicken pox. They were getting over them, but we still had to watch them. We were just about the same distance from home when, for the second day in a row the transmission went out. We were able to get to a gas station, but no further. It was hot, we were stranded, and the gas station attendants were shooting tin cans with a sawed-off shotgun in the parking lot. The kids were in the car. I could not even let them out;

I was mad as a hornet. I was not feeling or acting spiritual at all. I called the transmission shop and told them to send a wrecker to pick up "their" car. They sent one right away. I also called a friend who was in our church and asked if he would come and pick us up and he said he would leave right then. In the meantime, I continued to fume. I was not thinking spiritual thoughts.

After a few minutes, a man drove into the gas station in a pickup truck. He was not from Arkansas but was traveling through on Interstate 40. He pulled up to a gas pump, filled his truck with gasoline and was pouring oil into his engine. He seemed to be in as bad a mood as I was. I looked at him, and I said, "Isn't this something?" He said back to me, "You are a Preacher aren't you?" I replied, "How could you know that?" He then said, "That's why I didn't say any cuss words." I asked him, "Do you want to get saved?" He responded, "Yes I do." I then replied, "Pull your truck over there." That was the sum of our conversation. It was not planned or thought out. I was not dressed like a preacher, I was not acting like a preacher, nor was I thinking like a preacher at that moment, yet he knew I was one.

You may be laughing now, I am. God does have a sense of humor. It took two breakdowns in two days for me and a botched rebuilding of a motor for Him to get us both in the right place at the right time for him to trust Christ. When I sat with him in the cab of his pickup, he told me that his daughter had been praying for him. Leading him to Christ was easy. When he trusted Christ and I had finished sharing with him what had just happened, the tow truck arrived and our ride arrived at the same time. We both drove off rejoicing. By the way, the next transmission lasted until we gave the car away many years later.

I learned something from that experience. God is in control, and we can trust Him even when we don't understand what is going on. That day I was truly overcome by His love for me and that man.

I could share many more stories like these, but I am only going to share one more. I am going to share with you how God often uses normal relationships with people in your daily lives to bring Himself glory and to bring other people to Him.

There was a young man named Brian. He was the manager of a tire, oil and lube shop. Over the course of a year or so I had come to know Brian very well. He was married to a young lady from Mexico and I was traveling to Mexico a lot with Grace Walk Ministries.

He was going through marriage troubles, and we discussed it from time to time. Brian was the son of a Pentecostal preacher so he knew a lot of Christian terminology but He did not really know Christ, by his own admission. One day, I was buying tires and sharing with him who Christ was, what He had given him and that He loved Him unconditionally just as He was. As he was putting the last wheel on the car, I asked him if there was anything that would prevent him from trusting Christ right then and there. He said no and put the tire down, bowed his head and received

Christ. It was glorious. He was born again next to a car lift. There is no bad place to be saved. I did not go into the store thinking, "today I am going to lead Brian to the Lord". Over the next few months, I was able to give Brian tapes and counsel him about his marriage and his new life in Christ.

I hope you have understood what I have been saying. Being a witness is who you are and not what you do. You have died with Christ, and the life you now live is not yours at all. Your life is in Christ, and Jesus is your life, Col.3:4. Be who you are in Him. Relax and watch and see what great things He does. You will be amazed at what He will do through you.

This is real evangelism. You may be saying, "Nothing like this has ever happened to me." It may or it may not, that is not your problem. Just know who He is, know who you are in Him, and know that He loves you. He will take care of the rest. You cannot measure results, and you don't know the impact you are having on others. Remember the man at the gas station? He told me his daughter had been praying for him. He knew it because she had told him.

Remember one thing. Jesus loves people and He came to seek and save that which is lost. The Holy Spirit is the One who draws people to Jesus. It is His job to save folks, and He will do His job. I don't consider myself anything other than a fruit catcher. Just be who God made you, and let Him use you like He chooses, and enjoy your position in Him. People will say about you just what they did about the woman at the well in John 4. She had trusted Christ and told the men in the town that Jesus told her all things about herself. The men said they came to Christ because of the testimony of the woman, but they stayed because of Him.

It has always been about Christ, and it will always be about Christ. Trust Him in the area of witnessing in your life. Don't *try* to be a witness, know that you *are* a witness. Christ said it in Acts 1:8, "*But you will receive power when the Holy Spirit has come upon you; and* **you shall be My witnesses** *both in Jerusalem, and in all Judea and Samaria, and even to the remotest part of the earth.*" It is not about you; it is all about Him.

Chapter 10

Come to Me

Have you ever been tired or discouraged or just felt totally defeated? It sometimes seems that you are so low you would have to climb out of a twelve-foot deep ditch just to get into a valley. It may seem as if nobody cares or even knows what you are going through in your life. You may be asking the question, "Why is God *allowing* this to happen to me?" Or you may be, like Job, asking God, "Why are You *doing* this to me?" You may not even have a picture of Jesus as a loving God at all. Is this you, or has it been you in the past?

If you are asking the question, "Why is this going on in my life", I think now is the time to look at what Jesus is saying to you through your circumstances. Jesus is saying, "*Come to Me*." This may be the main theme of the Bible. When Jesus says *"Come to Me"*, it tells all. It is His desire to have us come to Him. Jesus said in Matthew 11:27, *"…And no one knows the Son except the Father; nor does anyone know the Father except the Son, and anyone to whom the Son wills to reveal Him."* Jesus has revealed the Father to you, and He has and is revealing Himself to you. He is calling you to Himself when He says, *"Come to Me."*

What do we know about Jesus? We know what Jesus said about Himself in the Bible. Jesus said in Matthew 11:28-30, *"Come to me all who are weary and heavy laden and I will give you rest. Take my yoke upon you and learn from Me, for I am gentle and humble in heart, and you will find rest for your souls."*

These verses tell us so much about our Lord Jesus. What He really wants from me is me. He desires for me to come to Him. When my children were small and they saw me; they would run to me. I can't tell you the amount of pleasure that this brought to me. It made my day. I didn't want anything from my children; I just wanted their presence. Having my children with me was a blessing to me, and it still is. Jesus wants us to come to Him. He is blessed by having us in His presence. We don't have to guess about this. He told us so when He said, "Come to me."

Jesus told us who it was that he wanted to come to Him. It was *all* who were weary and heavy laden. I'm going to share with you some intimate things about myself. Many times, when I come to Jesus or to the Father, it is because I am weary. This is not a physical weariness; it is when I am weary of my own doings. Sometimes, it is when I seem to lack direction in my life. It seems as if the things that I pursue so much of the time are not things that I really want to do. In fact, sometimes they are things that I hate. I can say with Paul, "The things that I want to do, I do not do, and the things that I don't want to do, I do." I can ask the question with Paul, "Who will deliver me from this?"

When I come to the Lord, it is often with a broken heart. I say to Him, "You are my only hope." I also say, "You said come to you if I was weary and heavy laden, well here I am." Have you ever said that to Jesus, if not, why not? Would you be honest with Him? Jesus wants you to know that you can trust Him. He said that He would in no way cast you out. What He wants from you is simply for you to believe Him. The question is, will you? I have come to this conclusion; I will believe Him.

Sometimes I feel like things are weighing me down. I feel heavy laden. Well, this is another clear indication that I am the one that should come to Jesus. Is this you also? I believe that if you're honest you will admit that you feel weary and heavy-laden much of the time. Jesus said that when we come to Him, He would give us rest. Don't you long for the rest that is yours when you come to Jesus? This is called soul rest; it is in knowing that He is mine, and I am His.

What do I mean when I say that He is mine? Let me try to explain this to you from my son's point of view when he was four years old. I was playing my guitar and singing for a group of four-year olds on a

Wednesday night. They were laughing and singing along with me, and my son was standing on a table beside me. Every so often he would stop singing and point at me and say to the rest of the children, "My Daddy, my Daddy." He was my son, but I was his Daddy. I belonged to him. As far as he was concerned, I was his.

Do you feel like Jesus is yours? If you don't, you don't understand Jesus. He has given Himself for you and He has given Himself to you. He likes you calling Him, *yours.* Let me ask you again, do you feel like Jesus is yours? If you do, you will quickly come to Him. You will be quick to jump into His arms, not only when you are hurting, but also out of sheer delight.

When my grandson was not quite two years old, he would get his B's and his P's mixed up. He would call me Bapa. I didn't mind because when He saw me, he would get excited and cry out, "Bapa, Bapa." He loved me because he knew that I loved him. When he is hurt, he wants to be comforted. When he was happy, he wanted to be hugged. It is the same way with me and Christ. He wants me to come to Him all the time.

Jesus said that He would give us rest. This is not the kind of rest that comes when you are physically tired and you put your feet up. This is the kind of rest that comes when you realize that everything is going to be okay. Jesus wants us to realize this; in Him, everything is going to be okay. Even when I really mess up, Jesus wants me to come to Him and to know that His love for me is unconditional. Romans 8:28 says, "*And we know that God causes all things to work together for good to those who love God, to those who are called according to His purpose."* This verse even applies when the problems that arise in my life are my fault.

In the flesh, we may say this can't be so. God will only cause things to work together for good when I don't mess up. If that's true, then what Jesus did on the cross was worthless. Jesus died for folks who mess up. There is something that I want you to know; you could not save yourself, nor can you keep yourself. You need Christ all the time. It is all grace; you can't, in your own power, live a life that is pleasing to God. What it is we do that pleases Christ is to believe Him, to totally trust Him with everything. We see in Hebrews 11:6, *"without faith, it is impossible to please*

Him." What causes us to mess up is when we try to live our lives in our own power, independently of Him. Jesus said, "*Take my yoke upon you and learn from me.*" What am I to learn from Him? I am to learn that He is gentle and humble in heart. The word gentle is only used 10 times in the New Testament. All 10 of those times are relating to the nature of Christ. In Matthew 5:5 it says, "Blessed are the gentle in spirit, for they shall inherit the earth."

Who are the ones that are gentle in spirit? They are the ones that have the Spirit of Christ living in them. You cannot be gentle in spirit in your own power. First Thessalonians 2:7 uses the word "gentle" to describe a nursing mother. A nursing mother loves her baby. She cares for her baby, she caresses her baby, she protects her baby, and she would die for her baby. This is exactly how Jesus feels about you. Not only is Jesus gentle, but He also has a humble heart. The word "humble" means lowly or meek. There is no one greater than Christ, but He puts others before Himself. Even though He is fully God, He chose to become sin and to die so that we might become the righteousness of God in Him and to give you His life and His reward.

The word "meek" has a connotation of power under control. A stallion, which has been broken, is said to have been made meek. The horse is then useful to his master when he has been broken, because he is under the master's control. Jesus chose to place Himself under the complete control of the Father. I choose to place myself under the complete control of Jesus. When I do this, I will have His rest. The Bible says that we are to humble ourselves before the Lord, and He will exalt us. When we humble ourselves, we are totally dependent on Him. As we totally depend on Him, He exalts us. Sometimes, a problem arises. People want to exalt themselves, they want to do God's job. When we do God's job of exalting ourselves, He will do our job of humbling us. This is not because He is mad at us; it is because He loves us and wants us to be totally dependent on Him for our own good.

Jesus finishes this passage by saying; *"You will find rest for your souls."* He said, *"My yoke is easy and my burden is light."* The original meaning for yoke is, "scales". You have been weighed in Christ, and you have been found to have worth. His value has become your value. You have as much weight, as far as God the Father is concerned, as Christ does. This is not based on what you do but on what He has decided. All I can say about that is "WOW"!" Boy, do we have a great God or what!

Jesus said that His burden is light. You can ask yourself the question, "Does my burden seem light?" If I am going to be honest, much of the time, my burden does not seem light. When I carry *anything* for long enough, it gets heavy. We have the idea that we are going to give only the big things to Christ; the things that we know will weigh us down. Let me give you an illustration. If you were walking on a long journey and you started out with an empty pack on your back, it would be light. Along the way, you might pick up one small rock at a time and place it in the pack and you continued that for the whole journey. In the end, the pack would be full and it would be unbearably heavy. This is what we do as we go through life. We carry things, large or small, that He never intended for us to carry. What is it that He never intended for us to carry? He never intended for us to carry anything. Your only part in this journey of life is to completely trust Him, to lay every care or burden on Him and totally depend on Him for everything.

I can use the illustration of when I was in the army on a 10-mile march carrying a full field pack along with a rifle. That can be very heavy when you start but when you end it is devastating. When you think you can't march another step a duce and a half truck, comes for you and your squad or platoon is told to load up, the march is over and we are going to ride. When you get on the truck what would be the first thing that you do? For me it was to lay my pack down. How silly it would be to continue to carry my pack when the truck would carry both of us and I could rest. That is exactly what Jesus wants me to do, lay my burdens down. He can carry both of us. This is "humbling yourself" before Him. When you are humble, you are dependent, your burden becomes His burden, and to you it is light.

I am afraid much of the time I don't depend on Him. I try, fail, cry and then fall before I depend on Him. My desire now is to quickly come to Jesus. I can come to Him, warts and all, and know that He will love me and not cast me away. He won't even say, "I told you so." He knows everything about me. He even knows the things about me that I don't want anyone to know. He loves me and He knows how much I need to be loved. All of this is true for you too, will you believe it? You can say to the Father, along with me, "Father, I am weary of self- effort, weary of trying to do what *I think You would want me to do.*"

Do you see the problem? You think that God thinks like everyone else. You think the Father is going to base His approval of you according to what you do rather than what the Father, Son and Holy Spirit think of you. What they did on your behalf is sealed in heaven and brings God's complete and unchanging approval of you. Ephesians 1:13,14 says, "*In Him, you also, after listening to the message of truth, the gospel of your salvation-- having also believed, you were sealed in Him with the Holy Spirit of promise, who is given as a pledge of our inheritance, with a view to the redemption of God's own possession, to the praise of His glory.*" He approves of you because you have been brought into the Godhead as an act of their will from eternity past.

He chose you before the foundation of the world, in love He predestined you to be adopted as sons. You have nothing to do with this; it was all from the Godhead because they love you. You have the family name and the family characteristics. You look like Him, and you think like Him. This is mind boggling to some but it is true. God the Father, God the Son, and God the Holy Spirit love you and approve of you. This has nothing to do with your effort. It is all because of the covenant that God the Father made with Christ the Son on your behalf.

I want you to now say with me, "Father, I am so glad that you love me and desire me. Because you desire me, I receive You and come to You. I acknowledge that you are my life. That you see me as perfect, holy, complete and transformed. I am the apple of your eye.

I am the pearl of great price that You purchased with all You had. You glory in me and You rejoice in me. I am someone with whom You desire fellowship. I am going to be mightily rewarded based of what You do through me and I will be in Your bosom for all eternity. If I ever forget any of these things, quickly remind me so that I will quickly come to You."

It is my desire and prayer that you believe what has been done for you and given to you is yours. That what has been done for and given to you has been done for and given to all men. Tell everyone you meet what has been given to them. The life of Christ has been given to and for all men, asks them to believe and receive what has been given to them.

Made in the USA
Columbia, SC
20 April 2023